• TRIPLE TESTED •
FOR YOUR SUCCESS EVERY TIME

These days, everyone seems busy all the time so we've created *Meals in Minutes* as the answer to your cooking prayers. You know that takeaway food is not the answer, because it's generally high in cost and low in nutritional value. So when you see how fast and easily you can make a meal that's both delicious and wholesome, you'll be inspired by and excited about *Meals in Minutes*, the recipe for simply good eating.

Pamela Clark

FOOD EDITOR

Meals in *minutes*

Contents

Roman tomato soup, page 12

Potato, bacon & spinach frittata, page 16

Old-fashioned crumbed chicken and mash, page 101

Chilli, chutney and coconut pork, page 113

Meals in Minutes...

Busy? Who isn't? But, if economy meals, expensive takeaways and just-add-water dishes leave you worrying about health and nutrition, this collection of delicious, healthy meals is the solution. Some of these recipes take only minutes to make, others can be prepared ahead. All come with a guarantee that fast food can be good food.

72
Do ahead and make it easy

Preparation ahead — a boon for busy people. We've included delicious meals that store superbly as well as quick feasts that can be made following a raid of the pantry.

Grilled seafood to go, page 79

BRITISH & NORTH AMERICAN READERS:
Please note that Australian cup and spoon measurements are metric. A quick conversion guide appears on page 119. A glossary explaining unfamiliar terms and ingredients begins on page 115.

Saving time, saving money

While both the freezer and microwave oven are indispensable tools for saving time and money, few people use each to its full potential.

Time-saving tips

Organise your weekly menu, then shop for it all at the one time.

A well-stocked pantry, refrigerator and freezer will ensure you will always have a standby meal.

When appropriate, double the cooking quantities and freeze half of the dish for another time.

Use your microwave oven to shorten cooking preparation time.

Dried herbs can be used instead of fresh: 1 teaspoon of dried is equivalent to 1 tablespoon of chopped fresh.

Use bottled crushed garlic, minced ginger, chopped chillies, and so on rather than fresh; or freeze appropriate quantities when you have excess.

Ask the butcher to trim or chop your meat purchases.

Leftover cooked rice and pasta freeze well and can be reheated quickly and easily in your microwave oven.

PANTRY BASICS

These suggestions are based on recipes in this book. Once jars or bottles are opened, secure the lids tightly and keep them refrigerated. Leftover canned food must be transferred to a non-reactive container.

PANTRY
anchovies
barbecue sauce
bay leaves
breadcrumbs
burghul
Cajun seasoning
canned artichoke hearts
canned chickpeas
canned four-bean mix
canned kidney beans
canned potatoes
canned salmon
canned soya beans
canned tomato puree
canned tomatoes
canned tuna
capers
cardamom, ground

caraway seeds
chutney
coconut milk and cream
coriander, ground
couscous
cumin, ground
curry pastes (green, Madras, red)
curry powder
dried fruit (apricots, sultanas, raisins, currants)
dried herbs (basil, mixed herbs, oregano, tarragon, parsley, chives, etc)
fish sauce
flour (plain and self-raising)
freekah
French onion soup mix
garam masala
honey
horseradish cream
mayonnaise
mustard (Dijon, seeded, powder)
noodles
nutmeg
oil (vegetable, olive, peanut and sesame)
olives, black
oyster sauce
paprika
pasta

pasta sauce
pesto
pizza base
plum sauce
polenta
red lentils
redcurrant jelly
rice (arborio, calrose, long-grain)
salad dressing
satay sauce
semolina
sesame seeds
soy sauce
stock cubes, powder or packets
sugar (brown and caster)
sumac
sun-dried tomatoes
sweet chilli sauce
Tabasco sauce
taco sauce
taco seasoning mix
tandoori paste
tomato paste
tomato sauce
turmeric, ground
vinegar (white wine, balsamic)
wine (dry red, dry white)
Worcestershire sauce
yellow split peas

REFRIGERATOR
butter/margarine
cheese (parmesan, cheddar, mozzarella, pizza cheese)
cream
eggs
milk
sour cream
yogurt

FREEZER
bacon
bread
nuts (almonds, pine nuts, pistachios, walnuts)
pastry (ready-rolled puff)
peanuts
stale breadcrumbs
vegetables

FRUIT & VEGETABLES
carrots
garlic
ginger
kumara
lemons/limes
onions
oranges
potatoes
tomatoes

Freezer know-how

Many of the recipes in the "In 30 minutes or less" section are suitable to freeze or can be made a day ahead.

When cooking soups, casseroles, stocks, cakes, biscuits, etc, cook double quantities and freeze half.

When freezing items individually (such as prepared fruit and vegetables), place a single layer of food on a tray or in a shallow pan. Place, uncovered, in the freezer until just firm, then transfer food to freezer bags, remove the air and seal.

Remove air from the package to be frozen so that the food does not dry out, discolour or develop off-flavours.

Label all packages and containers with content's name, weight or number of portions, and date made.

Cooked food such as casseroles, etc should stand, covered, at room temperature for 1 hour, cooled in the refrigerator, then frozen. Freeze only small quantities or in individual, meal-size portions.

If you do not own a microwave oven, thaw food in the refrigerator (allow 10 to 24 hours, depending on quantity of food).

Defrosted food not used immediately should be kept refrigerated.

Keep the frozen food turnover constant; don't freeze more of the same thing until you've used up the original. Square and rectangular-shaped packages are the most space-efficient.

Keep seasonings to a minimum; adjust to suit your taste at reheating stage.

WHAT CAN'T I FREEZE?

Salad vegetables cannot be frozen if they are intended for use raw.

Seasoned poultry and rolled meats are not suitable.

Custards and cream fillings tend to curdle on thawing.

Flour-based sauces separate and become thin on thawing.

Gelatine or jelly-like dishes separate when thawed.

Mayonnaise and creamy-style salad dressings tend to separate when thawed.

Meringues and meringue toppings tend to both split and weep when thawed.

PACKAGING

Plastic bags, oven bags and freezer bags are suitable for most types of food.

Plastic wrap is suitable for separating food layers, but does not provide sufficient protection for wrapping.

Food can be wrapped in foil and frozen; be certain the food is securely wrapped.

Plastic containers such as resealable ice-cream, cottage cheese and yogurt containers are suitable for use in freezing liquids and semi-solid foods.

Many casserole and baking dishes are suitable for freezer-to-oven-to-table use.

When using rigid containers, leave 2cm to 5cm space for expansion of the food when it freezes.

Microwave know-how

Commonsense is the main requirement when using a microwave oven. They are economical, easy-to-use and time-saving. They heat the food, not your oven or kitchen, and cut down on washing up by minimising the number of dishes used.

The golden rule for cooking successfully in the microwave oven is to undercook the food slightly, then increase cooking time until the food is cooked as desired. Don't forget to calculate the effects of standing time: most food continues cooking even after the microwave oven stops.

When removing plastic wrap, pull it towards you to prevent the escaping steam from burning you.

Shield corners of square or rectangular containers with foil to prevent overcooking.

Variations in cooking times are due to many factors: size, density and water content of the food; size and shape of the cooking vessel; placement of the food in the cooking vessel; and the age, wattage and capacity of the oven.

For even cooking, fish, chicken, vegetables, etc, should be cut in a similar size and thickness. Foods of uneven thicknesses such as carrots, chicken drumsticks, etc, should be positioned with the thickest part facing the microwave oven walls.

Microwave ovens as a rule do not cook evenly, so it is important to stir or reposition food during cooking.

Generally, if food needs to be turned, covered, stirred, etc, when cooked conventionally, then it is also necessary in the microwave oven.

Pierce membranes and skins of foods such as potatoes, tomatoes, etc, with a skewer or fork before placing in the microwave oven.

Do not attempt to deep-fry or shallow-fry in the microwave oven because oil temperatures cannot be controlled.

Do not attempt to boil eggs in the microwave oven.

SUITABLE COOKWARE

A large range of cookware is designed for the microwave oven, but most non-metal dishes are suitable. If in doubt about the suitability of a dish, stand the dish in the oven with a glass of water next to it. Cook on HIGH for 1 minute. If the dish remains cold, it can be used in the microwave oven; if, like the water, the dish gets hot, don't use it in the microwave oven.

Food cooks more evenly and faster in a shallow, straight-sided round or oval dish rather than in a deeper dish of the same capacity.

When using plastic wrap to cover food, use caution when you remove the cover as the steam can burn you. The safest way to remove the plastic wrap is to pull it towards you, letting the steam escape away from you.

Ring-shaped moulds ensure cakes cook evenly. To improvise, place a glass in the centre of a round dish.

When reheating food cover it so that it will retain moisture.

Oven bags are good to use in the microwave oven. Secure them loosely with a rubber band, string or a strip cut from the top of the bag itself. Don't use metal ties even if covered in paper, plastic or foil.

In 30 minutes or less

You'll be amazed at how many different and imaginative possibilities for a main course you can come up with when you may be short on time but are filled with enthusiasm. Most of these recipes call for fewer than 8 ingredients, many of which you'll already have on hand in your kitchen cupboard or refrigerator, and all of them can be made in less than half an hour — who says fast food can't also be good food?

PAN-FRIED GREEN PEPPERCORN CHICKEN

8 (1.2kg) chicken thigh cutlets
1/4 cup (60g) seeded mustard
2 tablespoons drained green peppercorns, chopped
2 cloves garlic, crushed
2 tablespoons lemon juice
1/4 cup chopped fresh chives
1/4 cup (60ml) olive oil
1 small (80g) onion, chopped

Remove and discard skin from chicken; place chicken in large bowl, coat with combined mustard, peppercorns, garlic, juice, chives and 2 tablespoons of the oil.

Heat remaining oil in large non-stick pan; cook onion, stirring, until soft. Add chicken to pan; cook, brushing chicken with peppercorn mixture occasionally, until chicken is browned both sides and cooked through.

SERVES 4

Tea-towel from Home & Garden on the Mall

SATAY CHICKEN BURGERS

Packages of pide, Turkish bread, can be found on the breadshelves of your favourite supermarket but, if at all possible, try a loaf of pide freshly baked from a Middle-Eastern bakery — it's absolutely delicious!

1 long loaf Turkish pide
750g minced chicken
1 cup (70g) stale breadcrumbs
1/4 cup finely chopped fresh
    coriander leaves
2/3 cup (160ml) satay sauce
1 large (180g) carrot, peeled
1 (130g) Lebanese cucumber
1 cup (250ml) yogurt

Quarter pide widthways; cut each piece in half horizontally. Place pieces, cut-side up, on oven tray; toast, on both sides, under heated grill until browned lightly.

Combine chicken, breadcrumbs, coriander and half the sauce in large bowl; shape into 4 patties. Cook in large heated oiled pan until browned both sides and cooked through.

Meanwhile, using a vegetable peeler, slice carrot and cucumber into thin strips.

Top each of the pide bases with a burger, equal amounts of carrot and cucumber strips, and combined yogurt and remaining sauce.

SERVES 4

COCONUT CHICKEN SOUP

60g dried rice stick noodles
$1/4$ cup (60ml) mild curry paste
**2 tablespoons finely chopped
    fresh lemon grass**
$1^2/_3$ cups (410ml) coconut milk
$3^1/_2$ cups (875ml) chicken stock
$1^1/_2$ teaspoons fish sauce
1 tablespoon lime juice
**3 (510g) chicken breast fillets,
    sliced finely**

Place noodles in medium heatproof bowl, cover with boiling water, stand until just tender; drain.

Cook paste and lemon grass in large heated dry pan until fragrant; stir in coconut milk, stock, sauce and juice. Simmer, covered, about 5 minutes or until heated through.

Add chicken; cook, stirring, about 5 minutes or until cooked through. Add noodles; stir until heated through.

SERVES 4

Bowl and plate from Accoutrement

WARM CHICKEN AND POTATO SALAD

2 tablespoons olive oil
1kg tiny new potatoes, halved
4 bacon rashers, chopped
1 large cooked chicken
$1/2$ cup (125ml) sour cream
$1/3$ cup (80ml) mayonnaise
2 tablespoons seeded mustard
$1/4$ cup finely chopped fresh chives

Combine oil and potatoes in large baking dish; bake, uncovered, in very hot oven 25 minutes, turning once during cooking.

Meanwhile, cook bacon in large heated oiled pan until crisp; drain on absorbent paper. Remove and discard skin and bones from chicken; chop chicken roughly.

Gently toss potatoes, bacon and chicken in large bowl with cream, mayonnaise, mustard and chives.

SERVES 4

Opposite above Satay chicken burgers
Left Coconut chicken soup
Above Warm chicken and potato salad

Soup bowl from Pillivuyt; yellow plates from Lifestyle Imports

PUMPKIN AND LEEK SOUP

40g butter
1 large (500g) leek, sliced
1kg butternut pumpkin, chopped
2 medium (400g) potatoes, chopped
4 cups (1 litre) chicken stock
$1/2$ cup (125ml) milk
$1/2$ cup (125ml) cream

Heat butter in large pan; cook leek, stirring, until soft.

Meanwhile, boil, steam or microwave pumpkin and potato, separately, until tender; drain. Mash pumpkin and potato together; stir into pan with leek mixture. Add stock and milk.

Blend or process mixture, in batches, until smooth. Return mixture to clean pan; stir over heat until heated through. Ladle soup into serving bowls; swirl cream into soup.

SERVES 4 TO 6

TOMATO, FETTA AND SPINACH GALETTES

There are many different bottled pestos on supermarket shelves these days; we chose a pesto flavoured with sun-dried tomatoes.

250g frozen spinach, thawed
2 sheets ready-rolled puff pastry
$1/3$ cup (80ml) bottled pesto
200g soft fetta cheese, crumbled
$1/4$ cup finely chopped fresh basil leaves
250g cherry tomatoes, halved
$1/4$ cup (20g) coarsely grated parmesan cheese
1 teaspoon cracked black pepper

Drain spinach then, using hands, squeeze excess liquid from spinach; chop roughly.

Oil 2 oven trays; place 1 sheet of pastry on each. Fold edges of pastry inward to form 1cm border; pinch corners of bases together. Divide pesto between bases; spread evenly to cover base. Top each with spinach, cheese, basil and tomatoes; sprinkle with cheese and pepper. Cook in very hot oven about 15 minutes or until crisp and browned lightly.

SERVES 4 TO 6

Above Pumpkin and leek soup
Right Tomato, fetta and spinach galettes

China from Pillivuyt

ROMAN TOMATO SOUP

1 tablespoon olive oil
2 cloves garlic, crushed
1 medium (150g) onion,
   chopped finely
445g can condensed tomato soup
400g can tomatoes,
   undrained, crushed
3 cups (750ml) water
2 cups (210g) small fusilli
   (spiral pasta)
1 tablespoon finely chopped
   fresh basil leaves
2 bacon rashers, chopped finely

Heat oil in large pan; cook garlic and onion, stirring, until onion is soft. Add undiluted soup, tomatoes, water and pasta. Bring to boil; simmer, uncovered, about 10 minutes or until pasta is just tender. Stir in basil.

Meanwhile, cook bacon in medium heated oiled pan until browned and crisp; drain on absorbent paper. Ladle soup into serving bowls; sprinkle with bacon.

SERVES 4 TO 6

Left Roman tomato soup
Below Chicken and basil Turkish pizza
Right Baked fetta and roasted
tomato pasta salad

CHICKEN AND BASIL
TURKISH PIZZA

You will need a large bottle of tomato sauce, sometimes labelled sugo, and a loaf of the Turkish bread called pide, both now available in most supermarkets.

2¹/₃ cups (600ml) bottled tomato
   pasta sauce
1 long loaf Turkish pide
¹/₂ cup firmly packed
   fresh basil leaves
2 cups (300g) cooked
   chicken, shredded
200g fetta cheese, crumbled
¹/₂ cup (40g) coarsely grated
   parmesan cheese
¹/₂ cup (50g) coarsely grated
   mozzarella cheese

Pour sauce into medium pan. Bring to boil; simmer, uncovered, about 5 minutes or until thickened slightly.

Meanwhile, halve pide widthways; slice through each half horizontally. Shred half of the basil.

Place pide pieces, cut-side up, on unoiled oven tray. Spread sauce over pide; sprinkle with the shredded basil, chicken, fetta and combined grated cheeses. Bake, uncovered, in very hot oven about 15 minutes or until cheeses melt and brown lightly. Serve sprinkled with remaining basil leaves.

SERVES 4

BAKED FETTA AND ROASTED TOMATO PASTA SALAD

We used penne in this salad but use any short pasta you like — try farfelle or fusilli.

300g firm fetta cheese, chopped
1/2 cup (125ml) olive oil
500g cherry tomatoes
375g penne
1/4 cup (40g) pine nuts, toasted
1/2 cup firmly packed small fresh basil leaves
1/2 cup (60g) seeded black olives, sliced

Place cheese on large piece of foil; bring sides of foil up around cheese, drizzle with 2 tablespoons of the oil. Enclose cheese in foil; place parcel at one end of shallow baking dish. Combine tomatoes with 1 tablespoon of the remaining oil in same baking dish. Bake, uncovered, in very hot oven about 15 minutes or until tomatoes are soft.

Meanwhile, cook pasta in large pan of boiling water until just tender; drain. Gently combine pasta with tomatoes, cheese and any pan juices in large bowl with combined remaining oil, pine nuts, basil and olives.

SERVES 4

Plates from The Bay Tree Kitchen Shop

CHILLI GINGER OCTOPUS WITH CRISPED VEGETABLES

1 medium (120g) carrot
1 small (150g) red capsicum
1.25kg baby octopus
**1 tablespoon finely grated
    fresh ginger**
1 tablespoon sweet chilli sauce
1/4 cup (60ml) barbecue sauce
1/2 cup (125ml) orange juice
**60g mesclun (mixed small
    salad leaves)**

Cut carrot into thirds crossways; quarter capsicum, discard seeds. Cut vegetable pieces into thin strips; place in small bowl. Cover with iced water; refrigerate.

Meanwhile, remove and discard heads and beaks from octopus; cut in half. Combine ginger and sauces in medium bowl with octopus.

Drain octopus over small bowl; reserve sauce mixture. Cook octopus, in batches, in large heated oiled pan until browned and tender. Cover to keep warm.

Add reserved sauce mixture and juice to same pan. Bring to boil; simmer, uncovered, about 2 minutes or until sauce thickens slightly. Return octopus to pan; stir until glazed and heated through.

Serve octopus with drained crisped vegetables and mesclun.

SERVES 4

GRILLED HALOUMI, TOMATO AND EGGPLANT SALAD

1/2 cup (125ml) olive oil
4 (240g) baby eggplants, sliced
**4 medium (300g) egg tomatoes,
    halved lengthways**
400g haloumi cheese, sliced thinly
250g rocket, chopped coarsely
**1/4 cup firmly packed
    fresh basil leaves**
2 tablespoons red wine vinegar
2 teaspoons chopped drained capers

Heat 1 tablespoon of the oil in large pan or griddle; cook eggplant until browned both sides. Remove from pan.

Add tomato to same pan; cook, cut-side down, until browned and softened slightly. Remove from pan.

Heat another tablespoon of the oil in same pan; cook haloumi until browned lightly both sides.

Combine eggplant, tomato, haloumi, rocket and basil in large bowl with remaining oil, vinegar and capers.

SERVES 4

Opposite Chilli ginger octopus with crisped vegetables
Above Grilled haloumi, tomato and eggplant salad

POTATO, BACON AND SPINACH FRITTATA

4 (800g) medium potatoes, peeled
1 tablespoon olive oil
**1 medium (150g) onion,
   sliced thinly**
4 bacon rashers, chopped finely
**8 large spinach leaves,
   shredded finely**
6 eggs
1/2 cup (125ml) milk
**1/2 cup (60g) coarsely grated
   cheddar cheese**

Cut potatoes into 2cm cubes. Boil, steam or microwave until just tender; drain.

Heat oil in large non-stick pan; cook onion and bacon, stirring, until onion is soft. Add potatoes; stir until browned lightly. Add spinach; stir until just wilted.

Whisk eggs and milk in large bowl. Pour egg mixture into pan; cook, tilting pan, over medium heat until egg mixture is almost set.

Sprinkle frittata with cheese; place pan under heated grill until cheese is browned lightly.

SERVES 4 TO 6

Placemat and bowl from Kitchen Kapers; wooden platter and salad servers from Intarsia Homeware; plates from Sirocco Homewares

Plates from Lifestyle Imports

BABY SPINACH, POTATO AND EGG SALAD

750g tiny new potatoes, halved
1/2 cup (125ml) olive oil
6 eggs
4 bacon rashers, chopped
200g baby spinach leaves
2 tablespoons white wine vinegar
4 anchovy fillets
**2 tablespoons coarsely grated
   parmesan cheese**

Combine potatoes and 2 tablespoons of the oil in large baking dish; bake, uncovered, in very hot oven 25 minutes.

Meanwhile, cover eggs with water in medium pan; bring to boil. Simmer, uncovered, 10 minutes; drain. Rinse eggs under cold water; peel and quarter.

Cook bacon in large heated dry pan until crisp; drain on absorbent paper. Gently toss bacon in large bowl with potatoes, eggs, spinach and processed remaining ingredients.

SERVES 4

SATAY BEEF
AND NOODLE STIR-FRY

Both packaged fresh Hokkien noodles (also called stir-fry noodles) and bottled satay sauce can be found in supermarkets.

500g Hokkien noodles
1 tablespoon peanut oil
750g beef strips
2 cloves garlic, crushed
350g satay sauce
**500g packet frozen Chinese
vegetables, thawed**
**1/4 cup finely chopped fresh
coriander leaves**

Pour boiling water over noodles in large heatproof bowl; separate noodles with a fork, drain.

Heat half the oil in wok or large pan; stir-fry beef, in batches, until browned all over and just cooked.

Add remaining oil to pan; stir-fry garlic until fragrant. Add satay sauce; stir-fry 1 minute. Return beef to pan with noodles and vegetables; stir-fry until heated through. Stir in coriander.

SERVES 4 TO 6

FETTUCCINE WITH ROLLED
OMELETTE AND VEGETABLES

250g fettuccine
1 tablespoon peanut oil
4 eggs, beaten lightly
500g asparagus, chopped
150g snow peas, sliced
2 tablespoons soy sauce
2 tablespoons oyster sauce
2 tablespoons sweet chilli sauce

Cook pasta in large pan of boiling water, uncovered, until just tender; drain.

Meanwhile, heat half the oil in wok or large pan; cook eggs, swirling, to form thin omelette. Remove omelette from pan. Roll omelette tightly; slice into rounds. Cover to keep warm.

Heat remaining oil in same pan; cook asparagus until almost tender. Add snow peas and combined sauces; cook, covered, 1 minute or until vegetables are just tender. Gently toss pasta and omelette rounds with vegetables until heated through.

SERVES 4

Above left Satay beef and noodle stir-fry
Left Fettuccine with rolled omelette and vegetables
Right Gnocchi with spinach, tomato and pine nuts

GNOCCHI WITH SPINACH, TOMATO AND PINE NUTS

Gnocchi are the Italian version of dumplings; the most common types are made of potato, semolina or ricotta and spinach. They are available, ready-made, from the refrigerated sections of your supermarket; we used a potato gnocchi here.

3/4 cup (180ml) cream
425g can tomatoes
3 cloves garlic, crushed
1/2 cup (75g) drained chopped
   sun-dried tomatoes in oil
1/2 cup (60g) seeded black
   olives, sliced
750g packaged potato gnocchi
500g spinach, chopped coarsely
1/2 cup (80g) pine nuts, toasted

Combine the cream, undrained crushed canned tomatoes and garlic in large pan. Bring to boil; simmer, uncovered, about 5 minutes or until sauce thickens slightly. Add sun-dried tomatoes and olives; simmer, uncovered, 2 minutes.

Meanwhile, cook gnocchi according to package directions; drain. Gently toss gnocchi, spinach and pine nuts with sauce in pan until spinach wilts and mixture is heated through.

SERVES 4

Chicken shortcuts

Pick up a cooked chicken on the way home from work and quick-as-a-flash transform it into a scrumptious meal. These fabulous dishes can be created from a purchased barbecued or char-grilled chicken — or from the leftovers from your Sunday roast. An average 1kg cooked chicken will provide about 2 1/2 cups (425g) of chopped skinless and boneless meat; each of these recipe suggestions makes enough for 4 portions.

Sweet chilli
chicken stir-fry

Tandoori chicken rolls

Heat 1 tablespoon olive oil in medium pan; cook 1 chopped onion and 1 crushed clove garlic, stirring, until onion is soft. Add 200g sliced button mushrooms; cook, stirring, until soft. Add 2 1/2 cups (425g) chopped cooked chicken and combined 2 tablespoons tandoori paste and 1 tablespoon yogurt. Divide mixture among 8 medium-size flour tortillas; roll into cigar shapes. Place, seam-side down, on oiled oven tray; bake, uncovered, in moderate oven about 10 minutes or until browned lightly and heated through. Serve with 3/4 cup (180ml) yogurt combined with 1 teaspoon cumin.

Sweet chilli chicken stir-fry

Cover 500g Hokkien noodles with boiling water, separate with fork, stand 5 minutes; drain. Stir-fry 375g frozen Oriental vegetables in wok or large pan with 1/2 cup (125ml) honey and chilli stir-fry sauce and 2 1/2 cups (425g) chopped cooked chicken until combined. Add noodles; stir-fry until heated through.

Chicken vegetable pie

Combine 2 1/2 cups (425g) shredded cooked chicken in large pan with 430g can cream of mushroom soup and 2 cups frozen mixed vegetables; cook, stirring, until heated through. Spoon mixture into unoiled pie dish; cover with 1 sheet thawed ready-rolled puff pastry, trim edges. Brush pastry with lightly beaten egg; bake in moderate oven about 40 minutes or until pastry is browned lightly.

Tandoori chicken
rolls

Chicken and bean bake

Place quartered cooked chicken in large ovenproof dish. Combine 2 1/3 cups (600ml) bottled tomato pasta sauce with 420g can four-bean mix in large bowl; spoon mixture over chicken. Top with combined 1 cup (70g) stale breadcrumbs, 1 crushed clove garlic and 1 tablespoon chopped fresh parsley. Bake, uncovered, in moderate oven about 40 minutes or until browned lightly and heated through.

Chicken noodle soup

Combine 430g can cream of chicken soup, 430g can cream of chicken and mushroom soup, 2 cups (250ml) water and 2 cups (250ml) milk in large pan. Bring to boil; simmer. Stir in 2 1/2 cups (425g) finely chopped cooked chicken and 85g packet 2-minute noodles; cook until heated through and noodles are tender.

Chicken and mushroom frittata

Heat 1 tablespoon olive oil in large pan; cook 3 finely chopped green onions and 200g thinly sliced button mushrooms, stirring, until soft. Add 1 medium (190g) chopped tomato; cook until most of the liquid evaporates. Stir in 2¹/₂ cups (425g) chopped cooked chicken. Pour 6 lightly beaten eggs over chicken mixture, sprinkle with 2 cups (250g) coarsely grated cheddar cheese; cook over low heat until just set. Place pan under heated grill until cheese melts and frittata is browned lightly.

Sun-dried tomato, pesto and chicken pizza

Halve 1 long loaf Turkish pide lengthways, place both halves on unoiled oven tray; spread with ¹/₂ cup (125ml) bottled pesto. Top with 2¹/₂ cups (425g) chopped cooked chicken, ¹/₂ cup (75g) chopped drained sun-dried tomatoes, 150g sliced button mushrooms and 1 cup (125g) grated cheddar cheese. Bake, uncovered, in very hot oven about 10 minutes or until cheese melts and pizza is heated through.

Chicken and
mushroom frittata

Chicken burritos

Combine 2¹/₂ cups (425g) finely chopped cooked chicken in large pan with 3 cups (750ml) bottled salsa and ¹/₂ cup (125ml) water. Bring to boil; simmer. Meanwhile, soften 8 medium-size flour tortillas in microwave (or wrap in foil and place in hot oven) briefly. Divide chicken mixture among tortillas; top with equal amounts 1 cup shredded lettuce, 1 cup (125g) coarsely grated cheddar cheese and 1 large (250g) finely chopped tomato. Roll into cigar shapes to serve.

Garlic chicken and
pasta salad

Chicken burritos

Garlic chicken and pasta salad

Cook 375g pasta in large pan of boiling water, uncovered, until just tender; drain. Place pasta in large bowl; stir in combined ¹/₄ cup (60ml) olive oil, 2 crushed cloves garlic and ¹/₃ cup (80ml) lemon juice. Add 4 finely sliced green onions and 2¹/₂ cups (425g) chopped cooked chicken; gently toss to combine.

Plate from Sirocco Homewares; fabric, bowl and chopsticks from Intarsia Homeware

VIETNAMESE BEEF AND NOODLES

750g whole piece beef rump, sliced thinly
1/4 cup (60ml) fish sauce
1/3 cup (80ml) oyster sauce
1/3 cup (80ml) sweet chilli sauce
3 cloves garlic, crushed
500g Hokkien noodles
2 tablespoons peanut oil
2 large (400g) onions, sliced
200g snow peas
80g bean sprouts

Place beef in large bowl with half of the combined sauces and garlic; cover, refrigerate 3 hours or overnight.

Pour boiling water over noodles in large heatproof bowl; separate noodles with fork, drain.

Heat half the oil in wok or large pan; stir-fry beef, in batches, until browned all over and almost cooked.

Heat remaining oil in same pan; stir-fry onion until soft. Add snow peas and sprouts; stir-fry 1 minute. Return beef and noodles to pan with remaining half of sauce mixture; stir-fry until mixture is heated through.

SERVES 4

PENNE BOSCAIOLA

The quill-shaped penne is a good pasta to serve with a rich, substantial sauce like a boscaiola or carbonara because the ridges on each piece of pasta help "trap" the creamy sauce and absorb its flavour.

375g penne
1 tablespoon olive oil
1 large (200g) onion, chopped finely
3 cloves garlic, crushed
4 bacon rashers, chopped finely
150g button mushrooms, chopped
300ml cream
1/2 cup (40g) coarsely grated parmesan cheese

Cook pasta in large pan of boiling water, uncovered, until just tender; drain.

Meanwhile, heat oil in large pan; add onion, garlic, bacon and mushrooms; cook, stirring, until onion is soft and browned lightly. Add cream to pan; stir until combined. Gently toss pasta and cheese in pan with mushroom cream sauce until heated through.

SERVES 4

Opposite Vietnamese beef and noodles
Below Penne boscaiola

Bowl from The Bay Tree Kitchen Shop

ASPARAGUS AND CHICKEN RISOTTO

300g asparagus, chopped
2 tablespoons olive oil
1½ cups (300g) arborio rice
1 clove garlic, crushed
1 litre (4 cups) chicken stock
**2 cups (340g) coarsely chopped
  cooked chicken**
**¼ cup (20g) coarsely grated
  parmesan cheese**
¼ cup (60ml) cream

Boil, steam, or microwave asparagus until just tender; drain.

Meanwhile, heat oil in large pan; add rice, stir about 2 minutes or until rice is coated with oil. Add garlic; cook, stirring, until garlic is just soft. Add hot stock, in batches; cook, stirring, over low heat until stock is absorbed between additions and rice is tender. Gently stir asparagus, chicken, cheese and cream into risotto.

SERVES 4

Chilli bottle from Accoutrement; bowls from Orson & Blake Collectables; tiles from Country Floors

STIR-FRIED NOODLES WITH CHILLI PRAWNS

600g Hokkien noodles
15 (750g) large uncooked prawns
1 tablespoon peanut oil
400g baby bok choy
2 tablespoons sweet chilli sauce
1/4 cup (60ml) chicken stock
2 tablespoons lime juice
1 clove garlic, crushed

Pour boiling water over noodles in large heatproof bowl; separate noodles with fork, drain. Shell and devein prawns, leaving tails intact.

Heat oil in wok or large pan; stir-fry prawns until just changed in colour. Add noodles, bok choy and combined remaining ingredients; stir-fry until bok choy just wilts and prawns are cooked through.

SERVES 4 TO 6

THAI STIR-FRIED PORK

750g pork strips
1/4 cup (60ml) green curry paste
115g fresh baby corn, halved
1 large (350g) red capsicum, sliced thinly
2/3 cup (160ml) coconut milk
11/2 tablespoons lime juice
200g baby spinach leaves
1/3 cup coarsely shredded fresh basil leaves

Cook pork, in batches, in heated oiled wok or large pan until browned all over. Cover to keep warm.

Stir paste into same pan; cook, stirring, until fragrant. Add corn and capsicum; stir-fry 2 minutes. Add milk and juice; stir-fry 2 minutes. Return pork to pan with spinach and basil; stir-fry until leaves are just wilted.

SERVES 4

Opposite above Asparagus and chicken risotto
Opposite Stir-fried noodles with chilli prawns
Above Thai stir-fried pork

SALMON AND SUN-DRIED TOMATO PASTA

375g farfelle (bow pasta)
3 (600g) Atlantic salmon fillets
2 tablespoons olive oil
1 large (200g) onion, chopped
3/4 cup (110g) sun-dried tomatoes
in oil, drained, chopped
300ml cream
1 cup (250ml) water
500g spinach, chopped
1/2 cup (40g) coarsely grated
parmesan cheese

Cook pasta in large pan of boiling water, uncovered, until just tender; drain.

Remove any skin and bones from salmon. Heat half the oil in large pan; cook salmon both sides, uncovered, until just tender. Remove from pan; flake salmon with fork.

Heat remaining oil in same pan; cook onion, stirring, until soft. Add tomatoes, cream and water; simmer, uncovered, about 5 minutes or until sauce thickens slightly. Add spinach and cheese; cook, stirring, until spinach just wilts and cheese melts. Gently toss pasta and salmon with tomato mixture in pan until heated through.

SERVES 4

RISOTTO MARINARA

2 tablespoons olive oil
1 medium (150g) onion,
chopped finely
2 cups (400g) arborio rice
3 1/2 cups (875ml) vegetable stock
30 (750g) medium
uncooked prawns
500g seafood marinara mix
1/2 cup (125ml) cream
1/2 cup (40g) coarsely grated
parmesan cheese

Heat oil in large pan; cook onion, stirring, until onion is soft. Add rice; stir about 2 minutes or until rice is coated with oil. Add hot stock; simmer, covered, for about 15 minutes, stirring halfway during cooking time or until liquid is absorbed.

Meanwhile, shell and devein prawns; discard heads and tails, cut in half through backs, combine with marinara mixture. Stir seafood into risotto; simmer, covered, about 7 minutes or until seafood is tender. Remove from heat; stir in cream and cheese. Stand, covered, about 2 minutes or until cream is heated through and cheese is melted.

SERVES 4

Below Salmon and sun-dried tomato pasta
Right Risotto marinara

Plates from Accoutrement

RISOTTO NAPOLETANA

2 tablespoons olive oil
1 large (200g) onion, chopped
1½ cups (300g) arborio rice
425g can tomatoes
3 cups (750ml) water
100g thin slices spicy salami,
    chopped coarsely

¼ cup (35g) sliced sun-dried
    tomatoes in oil, drained
½ cup (60g) seeded black
    olives, sliced
½ cup (40g) coarsely grated
    parmesan cheese

Heat oil in large pan; cook onion, stirring, until onion is soft. Add rice; stir about 2 minutes or until rice is coated with oil. Add undrained crushed canned tomatoes and water. Bring to boil; simmer, covered, 15 minutes, stirring once midway during cooking time. Remove from heat; stand, covered, 10 minutes. Stir in all remaining ingredients just before serving.

SERVES 4

TARRAGON FISH AND VEGETABLE PARCELS

We used blue eye here for its firm white flesh and succulent, delicate taste but any similar kind of fish will be suitable.

1 medium (350g) leek
1 large (180g) carrot
30g butter
2 tablespoons dry white wine
2 teaspoons chopped fresh tarragon leaves
4 (800g) white fish fillets

Cut leek and carrot into thin 4cm-long strips. Heat butter in large pan; cook vegetables, stirring, until softened slightly. Stir in wine and tarragon; cook, uncovered, 1 minute.

Place each fish fillet on a 30cm-square piece of foil; divide vegetables among fillets. Wrap tightly to enclose fillets, place on oven tray; bake in hot oven 20 minutes.

SERVES 4

CAJUN FISH CUTLETS WITH TOMATO CUCUMBER RAITA

Cutlets of blue eye (also known as trevalla) were used in this recipe.

1 tablespoon Cajun seasoning
1 tablespoon plain flour
2 teaspoons ground cumin
4 (1kg) white fish cutlets
200ml yogurt
3 (390g) Lebanese cucumbers, seeded, chopped finely
2 medium (380g) tomatoes, seeded, chopped finely
2 tablespoons lemon juice

Combine seasoning, flour and 1 teaspoon of the cumin in small bowl; sprinkle over fish. Griddle-fry (or grill or barbecue) fish until browned both sides and cooked as desired.

Meanwhile, combine yogurt, cucumber and tomato in medium bowl with remaining cumin and half the lemon juice. Drizzle fish with remaining lemon juice just before serving with tomato cucumber raita.

SERVES 4

RED CURRY LAMB CHOPS

2 teaspoons vegetable oil
8 lamb loin chops
1/4 cup (60ml) red curry paste
1²/3 cups (410ml) coconut milk
1¹/2 tablespoons lime juice
1 tablespoon brown sugar
2 teaspoons fish sauce
2 tablespoons finely chopped fresh coriander leaves

Heat oil in large pan; cook lamb chops, uncovered, until browned both sides and cooked as desired. Drain on absorbent paper; cover to keep warm.

Drain oil from pan. Add paste; cook, stirring, until fragrant. Stir in coconut milk, juice, sugar and sauce. Bring to boil, simmer, uncovered, about 5 minutes or until sauce thickens slightly.

Return lamb to pan; cook, uncovered, until heated through. Stir in coriander just before serving.

SERVES 4

Opposite Cajun fish cutlets with tomato cucumber raita
Top Tarragon fish and vegetable parcels
Below Red curry lamb chops

Pasta pronto

Making a pasta sauce needn't take hours: some don't even need cooking. Try using short or tubular pastas, such as penne, fusilli or shells, with some of these sauces because they hold ingredients better than the long, smooth ribbon-like pastas. Each recipe feeds 4 when served with 500g of pasta, cooked until al dente in a pan of boiling water.

Garlicky
toasted breadcrumbs
with a poached egg

Garlicky toasted breadcrumbs with a poached egg

Heat 1 cup (250ml) olive oil in large pan; add 3 cups (210g) stale breadcrumbs, 4 crushed cloves garlic, 1 tablespoon cracked black pepper, 1 tablespoon chopped fresh oregano and 1 tablespoon finely grated lemon rind, stirring, until breadcrumbs are brown and crisp. Gently toss breadcrumb mixture with hot pasta in large bowl; divide among serving plates, top each with a soft poached egg.

Capsicum, pesto and
white bean sauce

Capsicum, pesto and white bean sauce

Combine hot pasta in large bowl with 400g can rinsed and drained cannellini beans, 200g sliced roasted red capsicum, 3/4 cup (180ml) bottled pesto [we used a chargrilled-vegetable variety], 1/4 cup finely chopped fresh mint leaves and 1/2 cup (40g) coarsely grated parmesan cheese.

Smoked chicken, celery and pecan sauce

Gently toss hot pasta in large bowl with 1 1/2 cups (300g) chopped smoked chicken, 3 (225g) coarsely chopped trimmed celery sticks, 1/2 cup (50g) coarsely chopped toasted pecans, and combined 3/4 cup (180ml) mayonnaise and 1/3 cup (80ml) buttermilk.

Thai green chicken with broccoli and cashews

Karen's sauce Caprese

Combine 1/3 cup (80ml) olive oil, 1 medium (170g) finely sliced red onion, 1 crushed clove garlic, 1/2 cup finely shredded fresh basil leaves, 100g thinly sliced kalamata olives, 200g roughly chopped bocconcini cheese, 4 medium (760g) chopped tomatoes and 2 tablespoons finely chopped capers. Gently toss sauce with cooled pasta in large bowl.

Karen's sauce caprese

Thai green chicken with broccoli and cashews

Heat 2 tablespoons peanut oil in large pan; cook 2 teaspoons finely grated fresh ginger and 4 (680g) coarsely chopped chicken breast fillets, stirring, until chicken is browned all over. Add 1/4 cup (60ml) green curry paste, 11/2 cups (375ml) coconut cream, 300ml cream and 250g coarsely chopped broccoli; simmer, stirring occasionally, about 5 minutes or until sauce thickens slightly. Gently toss with hot pasta in large bowl; sprinkle with 1 cup (150g) toasted cashews.

Creamy mushroom and bacon sauce

Heat 1 tablespoon olive oil in large pan; cook 1 medium (150g) coarsely chopped onion and 4 thinly sliced bacon rashers until bacon is browned. Add 250g sliced button mushrooms; cook, stirring, until mushrooms are tender. Add 1/2 cup (125ml) dry white wine; cook 2 minutes. Stir in 300ml cream. Bring to boil; simmer, uncovered, 5 minutes. Gently toss sauce with hot pasta in large bowl.

Cauliflower blue cheese sauce

Boil, steam or microwave 3 cups (300g) finely chopped cauliflower until almost tender; drain. Combine 1 cup (250ml) sour cream, 1/2 cup (100g) crumbled creamy blue cheese and 2 crushed cloves garlic in small pan; stir over low heat until cheese melts. Gently toss blue cheese mixture and cauliflower in large bowl with hot pasta, 1 medium (170g) finely sliced red onion, 3/4 cup (100g) thinly sliced pimento-stuffed green olives and 2 tablespoons finely chopped fresh chives.

Creamy mushroom and bacon sauce

Below Saucy chicken in yogurt
Right Honey mustard veal chops

SAUCY CHICKEN IN YOGURT

750g chicken tenderloins
525g bottled satay sauce
2 large (400g) onions
1 tablespoon olive oil
250g cherry tomatoes, halved
1/3 cup shredded fresh basil leaves
200ml yogurt
2 tablespoons sweet chilli sauce

Combine chicken and 1/2 cup of the satay sauce in large bowl; stand 5 minutes.

Cook chicken, in batches, in large heated oiled pan until cooked through. Cover to keep warm.

Meanwhile, chop onions into wedges. Heat oil in same pan; cook onion, stirring, until soft. Add remaining satay sauce, tomatoes and basil; cook, stirring, about 5 minutes or until heated through.

Return chicken to pan; stir to coat with satay sauce mixture. Serve chicken with combined yogurt and chilli sauce.

SERVES 4 TO 6

HONEY MUSTARD VEAL CHOPS

2 tablespoons olive oil
3 large (600g) onions, sliced
20g butter
2 tablespoons brown sugar
4 (800g) veal loin chops
1/3 cup (80ml) honey
1/4 cup (60ml) Dijon mustard

Heat oil in medium pan; cook onion, stirring, until soft. Add butter and sugar; cook, stirring, until sugar dissolves. Remove onion mixture from pan; cover to keep warm.

Place chops with combined honey and mustard in same pan; cook for about 10 minutes or until browned both sides and cooked as desired. Serve chops with caramelised onion.

SERVES 4

BARBECUE-FLAVOURED CHICKEN AND ONIONS

2 tablespoons lemon juice
2 tablespoons brown sugar
1 tablespoon honey
1 clove garlic, crushed
1/4 cup (60ml) soy sauce
2 medium (300g) onions
1 large cooked chicken, quartered

Combine juice, sugar, honey, garlic and sauce in small jug. Chop onions into wedges. Place chicken and onion in shallow baking dish; pour over half of the glaze mixture.

Bake, uncovered, in moderately hot oven about 20 minutes or until chicken is crisp and heated through, brushing with remaining glaze mixture frequently.

SERVES 4

SNAPPER WITH A TRIPLE-CHEESE CRUST

We used snapper but you can use any moist, firm white fish fillet.

1 tablespoon Dijon mustard
1 cup (70g) stale breadcrumbs
1/3 cup (35g) coarsely grated mozzarella cheese
1/3 cup (40g) coarsely grated cheddar cheese
1/3 cup (25g) coarsely grated parmesan cheese
2 tablespoons finely chopped fresh parsley
2 cloves garlic, crushed
2 teaspoons Lemon Pepper Seasoning
4 (800g) snapper fillets
cooking oil spray

Combine mustard, breadcrumbs, cheeses, parsley, garlic and seasoning in large bowl.

Place fish on oiled oven tray; press cheese mixture onto fish, spray with cooking oil spray. Bake, uncovered, in hot oven about 15 minutes or until cheese browns and fish is cooked through.

SERVES 4

Left Barbecue-flavoured chicken and onions
Above Snapper with a triple-cheese crust

BALINESE LAMB CHOPS

1 tablespoon peanut oil
12 lamb loin chops, trimmed
2 small (160g) onions, sliced
1/2 cup (130g) crunchy
   peanut butter
1/4 cup (60ml) sweet
   chilli sauce
2 tablespoons lemon juice
2/3 cup (160ml) coconut milk
1/2 cup (125ml) water
1 tablespoon finely chopped fresh
   coriander leaves

Heat oil in large pan; cook lamb until browned both sides and cooked as desired. Remove lamb from pan; cover to keep warm.

Drain excess fat from pan. Add onions; cook, stirring, until browned. Add peanut butter, sauce, juice and combined coconut milk and water to same pan; cook, stirring, until sauce thickens slightly. Stir in coriander; return lamb to pan, coat with sauce.

SERVES 4 TO 6

CHICKEN AND POTATOES IN A MUSHROOM CREAM SAUCE

400g tiny new potatoes,
   unpeeled, halved
2 teaspoons vegetable oil
8 (1.2kg) chicken thigh cutlets
200g button mushrooms,
   coarsely chopped
2 cloves garlic, crushed
1/4 cup (60ml) dry white wine
300ml cream
2 tablespoons shredded fresh
   basil leaves

Boil, steam or microwave potatoes until just tender; drain. Cover to keep warm.

Meanwhile, heat oil in large pan; cook chicken, in batches, until browned both sides and cooked through. Cover chicken to keep warm.

Drain away all but 1 tablespoon of the pan drippings. Add mushrooms and garlic; cook, stirring, about 2 minutes or until mushrooms are browned lightly.

Add wine; cook, stirring, until liquid is almost evaporated. Add cream and basil; cook, stirring, until sauce thickens slightly.

Pat potato pieces dry with absorbent paper. Stir potatoes into the mushroom cream sauce until heated through; serve with hot chicken.

SERVES 4

Below Balinese lamb chops
Right Chicken and potatoes in a mushroom cream sauce

Bowl, jug and throw from Orson & Blake Collectables

Plates, napkin rings and napkin from Accoutrement; tea-towel from Orson & Blake Collectables

Bowl from Accoutrement

LEMON GINGER FISH FILLETS

We used blue eye here but substitute any moist,
firm white fish that you can obtain easily.

4 (800g) white fish fillets
80g butter
1 teaspoon finely grated
  lemon rind
2 tablespoons lemon juice
1 teaspoon finely grated
  fresh ginger
2 tablespoons finely chopped
  fresh parsley
3 green onions, sliced finely

Cook fish in large heated oiled pan until
browned lightly both sides and just
cooked through.

Meanwhile, melt butter in small pan;
add rind, juice and ginger, cook 1 minute.
Stir parsley and onion into butter sauce;
serve sauce over fish.

SERVES 4

MIXED VEGETABLE KORMA

1/4 cup (60ml) korma paste
1 tablespoon black mustard seeds
1.5kg butternut pumpkin, chopped
1/3 cup (65g) red lentils, rinsed
2 cups (500ml) vegetable stock
500g cauliflower, chopped
1/2 cup (125ml) reduced-fat cream
200g baby spinach leaves

Cook paste and seeds in large heated dry
pan until fragrant. Add pumpkin, lentils
and stock, bring to boil; simmer, covered,
5 minutes. Add cauliflower; simmer,
covered, about 10 minutes or until pumpkin is just tender, stirring occasionally.
Add cream and spinach; stir until spinach
just wilts.

SERVES 4

Opposite Lemon ginger fish fillets
Above Mixed vegetable korma

Take a can of fish...

These recipes, which can all be made using canned tuna and salmon interchangeably, are so delicious that mum's tuna mornay and salmon bake are liable to all but vanish into oblivion and these become the new family favourites. Each recipe makes 4 portions.

Neptune's pizza

Combine 1 tablespoon balsamic vinegar and 2 tablespoons olive oil in large bowl with 250g trimmed rocket and 1 tablespoon small drained capers. Cook large (25cm) pizza base, uncovered, in very hot oven about 7 minutes or until browned and crisp. Spread base with 1/4 cup (60ml) sour cream, sprinkle with 3/4 of 415g can drained and flaked salmon; top base with rocket mixture, sprinkle the remaining salmon over the top.

Salmon tortilla

Beat 8 eggs in large bowl; stir in 1/4 cup (30g) coarsely grated cheddar cheese, 1/4 cup (60ml) cream, 1 tablespoon finely chopped fresh basil leaves, 415g can drained and flaked salmon and 1/4 cup (35g) drained and sliced sun-dried tomatoes in oil. Heat oiled 20cm pan; cook egg mixture, stirring gently with fork, until almost set. Place under hot grill to brown top; cut into wedges to serve.

Neptune's pizza

Ginger seafood fillo rolls

Tuna and potato cakes

Boil, steam or microwave 4 large (1.2kg) potatoes until tender; drain. Mash potatoes in large bowl. Heat 1 tablespoon vegetable oil in small pan; cook 2 medium (300g) finely chopped onions and 2 crushed cloves garlic, stirring, until onion is soft. Stir in mashed potato, 1 cup (120g) finely grated smoked cheese, 1 beaten egg and 425g can drained and flaked tuna. Divide mixture into 12 patties; cook patties, in batches, in heated oiled non-stick pan until browned both sides and heated through.

Ginger seafood fillo rolls

Combine 415g can drained and flaked salmon, 2 teaspoons finely grated fresh ginger, 2 tablespoons finely chopped fresh chives and 2 tablespoons sweet chilli sauce in medium bowl. Melt 40g butter in small pan. Quarter 4 sheets fillo pastry; brush each piece with a little butter. Place 1 level tablespoon salmon mixture on each piece; roll to enclose filling, tuck in ends. Brush rolls with remaining butter; bake in moderately hot oven about 15 minutes or until browned. Serve with extra sweet chilli sauce.

Salmon and cream cheese bruschetta

Combine ¼ cup (60ml) olive oil and 1 crushed clove garlic in small bowl. Cut 30cm French stick into 1cm slices; brush one side each slice with oil mixture. Toast both sides. Combine 210g can drained and flaked salmon with ⅓ cup (80ml) cream cheese and ½ teaspoon finely chopped fresh dill in small bowl. Divide salmon mixture among bread slices; top with thinly sliced red onion, garnish with extra dill.

Salmon and cream cheese bruschetta

Niçoise salad

Boil, steam or microwave 150g trimmed green beans until just tender; drain. Combine cooled beans in large bowl with 1 bunch trimmed curly endive, 2 sliced hard-boiled eggs, 150g halved cherry tomatoes, 425g can drained and flaked tuna, 100g seeded black olives. Drizzle with combined ½ cup (125ml) mayonnaise, 1 tablespoon finely grated lime rind, 1 tablespoon lime juice, 1 tablespoon finely chopped fresh dill and 1 crushed clove garlic.

Panzanella with tuna

Gently toss 170g croutons, 1 medium (170g) sliced red onion, 1 medium (120g) sliced carrot, 3 medium (570g) seeded and sliced tomatoes, 2 (150g) sliced celery sticks in large bowl with 425g can drained and flaked tuna, ¼ cup (60ml) bottled Italian dressing and ¼ cup shredded fresh basil leaves.

Tuna tabouleh pockets

Panzanella with tuna

Tuna tabouleh pockets

Combine 425g can drained and flaked tuna with 300g tub tabboulleh in medium bowl. Split 4 small pocket pitta breads in half; open pockets. Divide tuna mixture and 1 small (100g) thinly sliced red onion among pitta; drizzle with combined ¼ cup (60ml) mayonnaise and 1 tablespoon lemon juice.

CHILLI LIME FISH WITH TOMATO AND ONION SALSA

Blue eye cutlets were used here but try other fish — cutlets, fillets or steaks —to serve accompanied by this piquant salsa.

1 clove garlic, crushed
1 tablespoon finely grated lime rind
2 tablespoons oyster sauce
1/2 cup (125ml) sweet chilli sauce
1/2 cup (125ml) lime juice
4 (1kg) white fish cutlets
2 medium (380g) tomatoes, seeded, chopped finely
1 medium (170g) red onion, chopped finely

Combine garlic, rind, oyster sauce, 1/3 cup each of the chilli sauce and juice in large bowl. Add fish; stir to cover with lime mixture. Cover; refrigerate 15 minutes.

Meanwhile, combine tomato, onion, and remaining chilli sauce and juice in small bowl. Cover salsa; refrigerate.

Drain fish; reserve lime mixture. Cook fish in large heated oiled pan, brushing with reserved lime mixture, until browned both sides and just cooked through. Serve fish topped with salsa.

SERVES 4

Below Chilli lime fish with tomato and onion salsa
Right Pork chops Valenciana

PORK CHOPS VALENCIANA

4 pork loin chops
1/2 cup (175g) orange marmalade
2 tablespoons mild chilli sauce
1 tablespoon cider vinegar
1 teaspoon finely grated fresh ginger
1 teaspoon ground cumin
3 green onions, sliced finely

Cook pork, uncovered, in large heated oiled pan until browned both sides and cooked through. Remove pork from pan; cover to keep warm.

Meanwhile, cook marmalade, sauce, vinegar, ginger and cumin in small pan, stirring, until sauce thickens slightly; stir onion into sauce. Serve sauce over pork.

SERVES 4

VEAL MARSALA

8 (720g) veal schnitzels
50g butter
1 large (200g) onion, sliced
1 tablespoon plain flour
1/4 cup (60ml) Marsala
3/4 cup (180ml) beef stock
**1 tablespoon finely chopped
fresh parsley**

Cook veal in large heated oiled pan, in batches, until browned both sides and cooked as desired. Remove veal from pan; cover to keep warm.

Add butter and onion to same pan; cook, stirring, until onion is soft. Add flour; cook, stirring, until mixture thickens and bubbles. Gradually stir in combined Marsala and stock; stir until mixture boils and thickens. Stir in the parsley. Serve veal with sauce.

SERVES 4

LAMB FILLETS
WITH TOMATO MINT RAITA

2 teaspoons ground cumin
2 teaspoons ground coriander
1 clove garlic
1 1/2 cups (375ml) yogurt
750g lamb fillets
**2 small (260g) tomatoes, seeded,
chopped finely**
**1 tablespoon finely shredded fresh
mint leaves**
1 tablespoon lemon juice

Combine cumin, coriander, garlic and half of the yogurt in large bowl; add lamb, coat with yogurt mixture.

Griddle-fry (or grill or barbecue) lamb until browned all over and cooked as desired, brushing with yogurt mixture occasionally.

Meanwhile, combine remaining yogurt, tomato, mint and juice in small bowl. Slice lamb; serve topped with tomato mint raita.

SERVES 4 TO 6

Opposite above Chicken, asparagus and chickpea salad
Opposite Veal Marsala
Above Lamb fillets with tomato mint raita

Yellow bowl and cruet from Home & Garden on the Mall

MANGO CHUTNEY LAMB WITH ROCKET SNAP PEA SALAD

1/3 cup (80ml) yogurt
1/3 cup (80ml) mango chutney
1/3 cup (80ml) mild chilli sauce
12 lamb cutlets
250g sugar snap peas
150g rocket, trimmed
1/4 cup (60ml) olive oil
2 tablespoons balsamic vinegar

Combine yogurt, chutney and sauce in large bowl.

Griddle-fry (or grill or barbecue) lamb, brushing with yogurt mixture frequently, until browned on both sides and cooked as desired.

Meanwhile, boil, steam or microwave peas until just tender. Rinse peas under cold water; drain. Toss peas and rocket in large bowl with combined oil and vinegar. Serve rocket snap pea salad with lamb.

SERVES 4

Above Mango chutney lamb with rocket snap pea salad
Right Lemon pepper schnitzel

LEMON PEPPER SCHNITZEL

8 (720g) veal schnitzels
300ml cream
1 teaspoon grated lemon rind
2 tablespoons lemon juice
2 teaspoons chopped fresh rosemary
1 teaspoon chicken stock powder
1 teaspoon cracked black pepper

Cook veal in large heated oiled pan, in batches, until browned both sides and cooked as desired. Remove veal from pan; cover to keep warm.

Add combined remaining ingredients to same pan. Bring to boil; simmer, uncovered, about 5 minutes or until sauce thickens slightly. Return veal to pan; coat with sauce.

SERVES 4

GRILLED FISH
WITH PARSLEY PESTO

*We used individual-size (about 350g each)
fresh bream for this recipe.*

**3 cups coarsely chopped fresh
   flat-leaf parsley**
2 cloves garlic, crushed
1/3 cup (80ml) olive oil
1/2 cup (125ml) buttermilk
**2 tablespoons coarsely grated
   parmesan cheese**
4 (1.4kg) whole small white fish

Blend or process parsley, garlic, oil,
buttermilk and cheese until smooth.

Remove and discard heads from fish;
make 3 shallow diagonal cuts both sides
of each fish. Place fish on oven tray,
brush with half of the pesto; cook under
heated grill (or griddle-fry or barbecue)
about 4 minutes or until almost cooked
through. Turn fish, brush with remaining
pesto; grill until cooked through.

SERVES 4

LEMON TARRAGON CHICKEN

80g butter, softened
**1 tablespoon finely grated
   lemon rind**
1 tablespoon lemon juice
**1 tablespoon finely chopped fresh
   tarragon leaves**
1 tablespoon brown sugar
**4 (1kg) chicken breast fillets
   on bone**
1 medium (140g) lemon, sliced
8 unpeeled garlic cloves

Combine butter, rind, juice, tarragon and
sugar in small bowl. Remove and discard
skin from chicken; make 3 deep diagonal
cuts across each piece. Press butter
mixture into cuts; spread remainder all
over chicken. Place chicken in shallow
baking dish, in single layer, with lemon
and garlic. Bake, uncovered, in very hot
oven about 20 minutes or until browned
lightly and cooked through.

SERVES 4

Opposite Grilled fish with parsley pesto
Above Lemon tarragon chicken

MADRAS PORK CURRY

1 tablespoon peanut oil
750g pork strips
1 large (200g) onion, thickly sliced
1/4 cup (60ml) Madras curry paste
1 cup (250ml) coconut milk
2 tablespoons finely chopped
  fresh mint leaves
1/4 cup finely chopped fresh
  coriander leaves
2 large (500g) tomatoes, quartered,
  seeded, sliced

Heat oil in large pan; cook pork, in batches, until browned all over and cooked through.

Add onion to same pan; cook, stirring, until browned lightly. Stir in paste; cook, uncovered, until fragrant.

Return pork to the pan with coconut milk, mint leaves, coriander and tomato.

Bring to boil then simmer, uncovered, about 10 minutes, stirring occasionally, or until curry sauce thickens slightly and mixture is heated through.

SERVES 4

CHICKEN BREASTS IN SPINACH AND FETTA SAUCE

2 tablespoons olive oil
4 (680g) chicken breast fillets
1 medium (150g) onion,
  chopped finely
2 cloves garlic, crushed
1/4 cup (60ml) dry white wine
300ml cream
125g firm fetta cheese,
  chopped roughly
250g spinach, chopped roughly

Heat oil in large pan; cook chicken, uncovered, until browned both sides and cooked through. Remove from pan; cover to keep warm.

Add onion and garlic to same pan; cook, stirring, until onion is soft. Stir in wine. Bring to boil; simmer, uncovered, until liquid is almost evaporated. Add cream and cheese; simmer, uncovered, about 5 minutes or until sauce thickens slightly. Add spinach; stir until spinach just wilts. Top chicken with sauce.

SERVES 4

Above Madras pork curry
Above right Lamb with avocado and red onion salsa
Right Chicken breasts in spinach and fetta sauce

LAMB WITH AVOCADO AND RED ONION SALSA

3 cloves garlic, crushed
1 tablespoon balsamic vinegar
1/4 cup (60ml) lemon juice
2 tablespoons olive oil
12 lamb cutlets
1 large (320g) avocado, chopped
1 medium (170g) red onion, chopped
1 tablespoon chopped fresh coriander leaves

Combine garlic, vinegar, 1 tablespoon of the juice and 2 teaspoons of the oil in large bowl with lamb. Cover; refrigerate for 10 minutes.

Meanwhile, combine remaining juice and remaining oil in small bowl with avocado, onion and coriander.

Griddle-fry (or grill or barbecue) lamb until browned both sides and cooked as desired; serve with salsa.

SERVES 4

GLAZED THAI CHICKEN

8 (1.2kg) chicken thigh cutlets
1/2 cup (125ml) sweet chilli sauce
1 tablespoon fish sauce
1 tablespoon peanut oil
1 tablespoon chopped fresh
    coriander leaves
2 tablespoons lime juice
2 teaspoons salt-reduced soy sauce

Place chicken in large pan of simmering water; poach about 8 minutes or until almost cooked through; drain. Griddle-fry chicken until browned both sides and cooked through. Pour combined remaining ingredients over chicken; cook for about 1 minute or until chicken is glazed.

SERVES 4

NORTH AFRICAN-SPICED FISH WITH CUCUMBER YOGURT

We used ling, also known as kingclip or rock ling, but use any firm, white fish you like.

- **1 (130g) Lebanese cucumber**
- **2 teaspoons ground coriander**
- **2 teaspoons ground cumin**
- **2 teaspoons finely grated fresh ginger**
- **1/4 cup (60ml) olive oil**
- **4 (800g) white fish fillets**
- **200ml yogurt**
- **2 teaspoons finely chopped fresh mint leaves**

Grate cucumber coarsely; drain in sieve 5 minutes.

Meanwhile, combine coriander, cumin, ginger and oil in small bowl. Brush fish with spice mixture; griddle-fry (or grill or barbecue) until browned both sides and just cooked through.

Combine cucumber with yogurt and mint in small bowl; serve over fish.

SERVES 4

PEPPER STEAK WITH BALSAMIC BROWNED ONIONS

- **1 teaspoon cracked black pepper**
- **2 tablespoons finely chopped fresh parsley**
- **4 (800g) beef sirloin steaks**
- **1/4 cup (60ml) olive oil**
- **2 large (400g) onions, sliced**
- **2 tablespoons balsamic vinegar**
- **1 tablespoon drained chopped sun-dried tomatoes in oil**
- **2 cloves garlic, crushed**

Press pepper and parsley into beef; stand, covered, while cooking onions.

Heat 1 tablespoon of the oil in large pan; cook onions, stirring, about 10 minutes or until just brown. Add 1 tablespoon of the vinegar; cook, stirring, another 5 minutes or until onions caramelise. Remove from pan; cover to keep warm. Combine remaining oil and vinegar in small jar with tomatoes and garlic; shake well.

Griddle-fry (or grill or barbecue) beef until browned both sides and cooked as desired. Serve beef with browned onions; drizzle with dressing.

SERVES 4

Opposite Glazed Thai chicken
Above North African-spiced fish with cucumber yogurt
Right Pepper steak with balsamic browned onions

Beef

A tasty beef mince recipe reveals, under delicious cross-examination, 3 totally different disguises that will surprise family and friends.

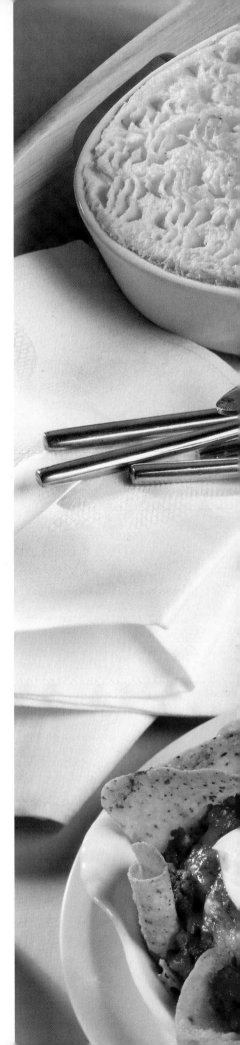

BASIC BEEF MIXTURE

One quantity of this recipe makes enough for the 3 dishes pictured here.

2 tablespoons olive oil
2 large (400g) onions, chopped
4 cloves garlic, crushed
2kg minced beef
3/4 cup (180ml) tomato paste
4 cups (1 litre) beef stock
4 bay leaves

Heat oil in large pan; cook onions and garlic, stirring, until onions are soft. Add beef; cook, stirring, until well browned. Add paste, stock and leaves. Bring to boil; simmer gently, uncovered, about 2 hours or until mixture thickens. [can be prepared ahead to this point and refrigerated overnight or frozen, in 3 equal portions]

BOLOGNESE SAUCE

1/3 portion Basic Beef Mixture
400g can tomatoes
1/4 cup (60ml) dry red wine
2 tablespoons tomato paste
2 tablespoons finely chopped fresh oregano
500g penne

Combine Basic Beef Mixture in large pan with undrained crushed tomatoes, wine, paste and oregano. Bring to boil; simmer, uncovered, about 10 minutes or until sauce thickens slightly. [can be prepared ahead to this point; refrigerate overnight or freeze]

Cook pasta in large pan of boiling water, uncovered, until just tender; drain.

Serve Bolognese Sauce with hot pasta.

SERVES 4

COTTAGE PIE

1/3 portion Basic Beef Mixture
1/4 cup (60ml) tomato sauce
1 tablespoon Worcestershire sauce
2 cups (240g) frozen mixed vegetables, thawed
4 medium (800g) potatoes, chopped roughly
60g butter

Combine Basic Beef Mixture in large pan with sauces and vegetables. Bring to boil; simmer, uncovered, about 10 minutes or until pie filling thickens slightly. [can be prepared ahead to this point; refrigerate overnight or freeze]

Spoon pie filling into 1.5-litre (6-cup) oiled ovenproof dish.

Boil, steam or microwave potatoes until tender; drain. Mash potatoes with half of the butter until smooth; drop spoonfuls of mash over beef mixture. Brush with remaining melted butter; place pie under heated grill until top is browned lightly.

SERVES 4

NACHOS

1/3 portion Basic Beef Mixture
1 teaspoon ground cumin
425g can pinto beans with chilli sauce
1 medium (250g) avocado
2 teaspoons lime juice
1 teaspoon Tabasco sauce
250g plain corn chips
1 cup (125g) coarsely grated cheddar cheese
1/2 cup (125ml) sour cream
1/2 cup (125ml) bottled salsa

Combine Basic Beef Mixture in large pan with cumin and beans. Bring to boil; simmer, uncovered, about 10 minutes or until mixture thickens. [can be prepared ahead to this point; refrigerate overnight or freeze]

Blend or process avocado, juice and sauce until just pureed. Cover tightly; refrigerate until required.

Divide corn chips among 4 flameproof dishes; spoon equal amounts of beef mixture over chips, sprinkle with equal amounts of cheese. Place dishes on oven tray; grill until cheese melts. Top Nachos with sour cream, salsa and avocado.

SERVES 4

Clockwise from top Cottage pie; Bolognese sauce with penne; Nachos

Lamb

Take 1 basic lamb recipe, divide into 3 different dishes and add up the compliments.

BASIC LAMB MIXTURE

One quantity of this recipe makes enough for the 3 dishes pictured here.

2kg minced lamb
1 large (200g) onion, chopped finely
2 cups (140g) stale breadcrumbs
2 eggs, beaten
3 cloves garlic, crushed

Combine all ingredients in medium bowl. [can be prepared ahead to this point; refrigerate overnight or freeze, in 3 equal portions]

THYME MEATBALLS WITH SPAGHETTI

1/3 portion Basic Lamb Mixture
1/4 cup (30g) seeded black olives, chopped finely
2 tablespoons tomato paste
1 tablespoon chopped fresh thyme
500g spaghetti

TOMATO SAUCE

1 tablespoons olive oil
1 medium (150g) onion, chopped
2 cloves garlic, crushed
2 x 400g cans tomatoes
2 tablespoons tomato paste
1/4 cup (60ml) dry red wine
3 teaspoons sugar

Combine Basic Lamb Mixture in medium bowl with olives, paste and thyme; roll level tablespoons of mixture into meatballs. Place meatballs on oiled oven tray, coat lightly with cooking oil spray; bake, uncovered, in hot oven about 15 minutes or until cooked through. Stir meatballs gently into hot Tomato Sauce. [can be prepared ahead to this point; refrigerate overnight or freeze]
  Cook pasta in large pan of boiling water, uncovered, until just tender; drain.
  Serve meatballs in sauce with hot spaghetti.

Tomato Sauce Heat oil in medium pan; cook onion and garlic, stirring, until soft and browned lightly. Add undrained crushed tomatoes, paste, wine and sugar. Bring to boil; simmer, uncovered, about 10 minutes or until sauce thickens slightly.

SERVES 4

TURKISH KOFTA WITH MINT YOGURT

1/3 portion Basic Lamb Mixture
1 tablespoon sumac
2 teaspoons ground cumin
2 teaspoons ground coriander
2 tablespoons chopped fresh mint leaves
2 teaspoons finely grated lemon rind

MINT YOGURT

200ml yogurt
2 tablespoons chopped fresh mint leaves
2 teaspoons finely grated lemon rind
2 teaspoons lemon juice
1 tablespoon tahini
1 clove garlic, crushed
1 1/2 teaspoons sugar

Combine Basic Lamb Mixture in medium bowl with spices, mint and rind; shape level tablespoons of mixture into oval-shaped kofta (you should have 36). Thread 3 kofta on each of 12 skewers; cook skewers on heated oiled griddle (or grill or barbecue), in batches, until browned all over and cooked through. Serve with Mint Yogurt.

Mint Yogurt Combine all ingredients in small bowl.

SERVES 4 TO 6

SUMMERTIME LAMBURGERS

There are many different-flavoured bottled pestos on the market; we used basil and roasted capsicum pesto here but try several until you find one you like best.

1/3 portion Basic Lamb Mixture
1/4 cup (60ml) pesto
1/3 cup (25g) coarsely grated parmesan cheese
2 tablespoons finely chopped fresh oregano
1 long loaf Turkish pide
125g baby rocket leaves
1 small (160g) avocado, sliced
1 small (100g) red onion, sliced finely
1 medium (190g) tomato, sliced

PESTO CREAM

2 tablespoons pesto
2/3 cup (160ml) sour light cream
2 teaspoons water

Combine Basic Lamb Mixture in large bowl with pesto, cheese and oregano. Shape into 4 patties; cook on heated oiled griddle (or grill or barbecue) until browned both sides and cooked through.
  Meanwhile, quarter pide; split pieces in half, toast both sides. Spread pide bases with some of the Pesto Cream; top with rocket, patties, avocado, onion, tomato and more Pesto Cream before covering with pide tops.

Pesto Cream Mix all ingredients in small bowl.

MAKES 4

Clockwise from top left Summertime lamburgers; Thyme meatballs with spaghetti; Turkish kofta with mint yogurt

Glasses, rack and plain plates from House in Newtown

Chicken

As easy as falling off your bike, making 3 different main courses from a single luscious chicken and mushroom mixture is child's play.

BASIC CHICKEN MIXTURE

One quantity of this recipe makes enough for the 3 dishes pictured here.

2.5kg chicken thigh fillets
1/4 cup (60ml) olive oil
3 medium (1kg) leeks, sliced
6 cloves garlic, crushed
1/4 cup (50g) plain flour
2 1/2 cups (625ml) chicken stock
1 tablespoon seeded mustard
300ml cream
375g button mushrooms, chopped

Cut chicken into 2cm pieces. Heat 2 tablespoons of the oil in large pan; cook chicken, in batches, until browned all over. Heat remaining oil in same pan; cook leeks and garlic, stirring, until leeks are soft. Add flour; cook, stirring, until mixture thickens and bubbles. Gradually stir in stock, mustard and cream; stir until mixture boils and thickens. Add chicken and mushrooms. Bring to boil; simmer, uncovered, 15 minutes. [can be prepared ahead to this point; refrigerate overnight or freeze, in 3 equal portions]

CHICKEN BOSCAIOLA WITH FETTUCCINE

3 bacon rashers, chopped
1/3 portion Basic Chicken Mixture
1/2 cup (125ml) cream
1/2 cup (125ml) water
1/4 cup (20g) coarsely grated parmesan cheese
1/4 cup shredded fresh basil leaves
375g fettuccine

Cook bacon in heated pan until crisp; drain on absorbent paper. Combine bacon with Basic Chicken Mixture, cream and water; cook, stirring, until sauce is heated through. Stir in cheese and basil. [can be prepared ahead to this point; refrigerate overnight or freeze]
Cook pasta in large pan of boiling water, uncovered, until just tender; drain.
Serve chicken sauce with hot pasta.

SERVES 4

CHICKEN AND VEGETABLE CASSEROLE

1/3 portion Basic Chicken Mixture
2 medium (240g) carrots, chopped
2 medium (400g) potatoes, chopped
2 tablespoons finely chopped fresh parsley
1/2 cup (60g) frozen peas, thawed
1/2 cup (125ml) chicken stock

Combine Basic Chicken Mixture in medium pan with carrots and potatoes. Bring to boil; simmer, covered, until vegetables are just tender. Stir in parsley, peas and stock; cook, stirring, until heated through. [can be prepared ahead to this point; refrigerate overnight or freeze]

SERVES 4

CREAMY CHICKEN AND MUSHROOM SOUP

1/3 portion Basic Chicken Mixture
2 (150g) celery sticks, chopped
2 medium (250g) parsnips, chopped
1 cup (100g) chopped cauliflower
3 cups (750ml) chicken stock

Combine Basic Chicken Mixture in medium pan with remaining ingredients. Bring to boil; simmer, covered, until vegetables are just tender. [can be prepared ahead to this point; refrigerate overnight or freeze]

SERVES 4

Clockwise from top left Chicken and vegetable casserole; Chicken boscaiola with fettuccine; Creamy chicken and mushroom soup

Do ahead and make it easy

Preparing a recipe to near-completion stage earlier in the week when you have the time is a great way to cook. Either freeze or refrigerate the dish as we've instructed in the recipes, then when required add the finishing touches, reheat and eat. And, because you've done the preparation long before meal-time, you'll find that the food is as good for the cook as it is for the gathering.

CURRIED LEEK AND KUMARA SOUP

1 tablespoon vegetable oil
1 medium (150g) onion,
   chopped roughly
2 large (1kg) leeks,
   chopped roughly
2 tablespoons curry powder
4 large (2kg) kumara,
   chopped roughly
2.5 litres (10 cups) chicken stock
2 bacon rashers, chopped finely
1/3 cup (80ml) yogurt

Heat oil in large pan; cook onion and leek, stirring, until leek softens. Add curry powder; cook, stirring, 1 minute.

Add kumara and stock. Bring to boil; simmer, covered, about 15 minutes or until kumara is just tender. Blend or process mixture, in batches, until smooth. [can be prepared ahead to this point; refrigerate overnight or freeze]

Cook bacon in small heated dry pan, stirring, until browned and crisp; drain on absorbent paper.

Cook soup in large pan until heated through; serve topped with yogurt and sprinkled with bacon.

SERVES 4

LEMONY LENTIL AND COCONUT SOUP

2 medium (300g) onions, chopped
1¹/₂ tablespoons ground cumin
1¹/₂ tablespoons ground coriander
2 teaspoons garam masala
2 medium (400g) potatoes,
  chopped coarsely
³/₄ cup (150g) yellow split peas
²/₃ cup (130g) red lentils
1.75 litres (7 cups) vegetable stock
1 cup (250ml) coconut milk
¹/₄ cup (60ml) lemon juice

Cook onion in large oiled pan, stirring, until soft. Add spices; cook, stirring, about 1 minute or until fragrant. Add potato, peas, lentils and stock. Bring to boil; simmer, covered, about 1 hour or until peas are tender. [can be prepared ahead to this point; refrigerate overnight or freeze]

Blend or process lentil mixture, in batches, until smooth; return to same pan. Stir in coconut milk and juice; reheat without boiling.

SERVES 4 TO 6

CHICKEN AND CREAMED VEGETABLE SOUP

1.25 litres (5 cups) chicken stock
3 medium (360g) carrots, chopped
1 stick (75g) celery, chopped
1 large (300g) swede, chopped
1 medium (150g) onion, chopped
2 bay leaves
4 (440g) chicken thigh
**   fillets, chopped**

Combine stock, carrot, celery, swede, onion and bay leaves in large pan. Bring to boil; simmer, covered, for about 20 minutes or until vegetables are tender. Discard bay leaves.

Blend or process vegetable mixture, in batches, until pureed; return mixture to same pan, add chicken. Bring to boil; simmer, uncovered, until chicken is cooked through. [can be prepared ahead to this point; refrigerate overnight or freeze]

SERVES 4

Underplate, napkins and butter dish from Accoutrement

LAMB SHANK AND VEGETABLE SOUP

1 tablespoon olive oil
4 (1kg) lamb shanks
1 medium (200g) onion, chopped
2 (150g) celery sticks, sliced
2 small (140g) carrots,
**   chopped coarsely**
1 medium (125g) parsnip,
**   chopped coarsely**
1 medium (225g) swede,
**   chopped coarsely**
1 medium (200g) potato,
**   chopped coarsely**
2 x 400g cans tomatoes
2 tablespoons Worcestershire sauce
2 litres (8 cups) water

Heat oil in large pan; cook lamb shanks, uncovered, until well browned all over. Remove from pan. Place onion, celery, carrot, parsnip, swede and potato in same pan; cook, stirring, until onion is soft.

Return shanks to pan with undrained crushed tomatoes, sauce and water. Bring to boil; simmer, covered, 2 hours, stirring occasionally. Cool; refrigerate overnight.

Remove and discard fat from soup. Remove shanks; cut meat from bones, discard bones. Chop lamb meat roughly; return meat to soup. [can be prepared ahead to this point; refrigerate for up to 2 days or freeze]

Bring soup to boil; simmer about 15 minutes or until heated through.

SERVES 4

Opposite above Lemony lentil and coconut soup
Opposite Lamb shank and vegetable soup
Above Chicken and creamed vegetable soup

China from House In Newtown

CHICKEN AND SPINACH SOUP

- **2 tablespoons olive oil**
- **8 (880g) chicken thigh fillets, chopped**
- **2 bacon rashers, chopped**
- **1 medium (200g) onion, chopped**
- **2 (150g) celery sticks, sliced**
- **1 clove garlic, crushed**
- **2 large (600g) potatoes, chopped**
- **2 litres (8 cups) chicken stock**
- **500g spinach, trimmed**
- **1/2 cup (125ml) cream**

Heat oil in large pan; cook chicken, in batches, until browned all over. Add bacon to same pan; cook, stirring, until crisp. Drain bacon on absorbent paper.

Add onion, celery, garlic and potato to same pan; cook, stirring, until onion is soft. Add stock, bring to boil; simmer, covered, about 15 minutes or until potato is just tender. Add spinach; cook, stirring, until just wilted. Blend or process vegetable mixture, in batches, until pureed.

Return soup to pan. Add chicken and bacon; cook, stirring, until chicken is cooked through. [can be prepared ahead to this point; refrigerate overnight or freeze]

Add cream; stir until heated through.

SERVES 4

SPRING VEGETABLE SOUP

- **2 tablespoons vegetable oil**
- **1 large (200g) onion, chopped**
- **2 cloves garlic, crushed**
- **1 medium (350g) leek, sliced**
- **2 medium (240g) carrots, sliced**
- **2 (150g) celery sticks, sliced**
- **200g button mushrooms, chopped**
- **1.25 litres (6 cups) vegetable stock**
- **50g spaghettini (or any fine pasta)**
- **1 tablespoon finely chopped fresh parsley**

Heat oil in large pan; cook onion and garlic, stirring, until onion is soft. Add leek, carrot and celery; cook, stirring, until vegetables are soft. Add mushrooms; cook, stirring, 1 minute. Add stock to pan. Bring to boil; simmer, uncovered, 15 minutes. [can be prepared ahead to this point; refrigerate up to 2 days or freeze]

Add pasta; cook, uncovered, until just tender. Stir parsley into soup.

SERVES 4

Above Chicken and spinach soup
Right Spring vegetable soup

COCONUT PRAWN BURGERS WITH MANGO SALSA

3/4 cup (150g) calrose rice
1²/₃ cups (410ml) canned coconut cream
1/2 cup (125ml) water
1kg medium uncooked prawns
1 tablespoon red curry paste
1 egg, beaten
1/3 cup (50g) rice flour
2 large (1.2kg) mangoes, chopped finely
1 small (100g) red onion, chopped finely
1/4 cup finely chopped fresh coriander leaves
1/4 cup (60ml) lime juice

Combine rice, coconut cream and water in medium pan. Bring to boil; simmer, covered tightly, about 15 minutes or until rice is tender and liquid absorbed.

Shell and devein prawns; discard heads and tails. Chop prawn meat coarsely; combine in medium bowl with rice mixture, paste, egg and flour. Cover; refrigerate 30 minutes. [can be prepared ahead to this point; refrigerate overnight or freeze]

Shape prawn mixture into 12 patties; cook, in batches, in large heated oiled pan until browned both sides and cooked through. Drain on absorbent paper.

Meanwhile, combine remaining ingredients in small bowl; serve salsa with prawn burgers.

SERVES 4

Right Coconut prawn burgers with mango salsa
Far right Grilled seafood to go

GRILLED SEAFOOD TO GO

20 (500g) medium
    uncooked prawns
400g baby octopus
2 cloves garlic, crushed
$1/2$ teaspoon sweet paprika
$1/4$ cup (60ml) balsamic vinegar
2 tablespoons tomato paste
300g scallops
1 long loaf Turkish pide
2 tablespoons olive oil
1 bunch rocket, trimmed

Shell and devein prawns, leaving tails intact. Remove and discard heads and beaks from octopus; cut in half.

Mix garlic, paprika, 2 tablespoons of the vinegar and paste in medium bowl. Add prawns, octopus and scallops; coat with marinade. Cover; refrigerate 3 hours or overnight. [can be prepared ahead to this point and frozen]

Cook seafood in large heated oiled pan, in batches, until the prawns change colour, and both octopus and scallops are tender and cooked as desired.

Meanwhile, quarter pide; cut each piece in half horizontally. Toast pide pieces both sides. Gently toss remaining vinegar with oil and rocket in large bowl; top toasted bread pieces with rocket and seafood just before serving.

SERVES 4

Plates and cruet set from The Design Store, glass from Home & Garden on the Mall

CHICKEN AND VEGETABLES IN TARRAGON CREAM

7 (770g) chicken thigh fillets, chopped
30g butter
250g asparagus, chopped
1 medium (350g) leek, sliced
1 large (180g) carrot, chopped
2 tablespoons plain flour
1 cup (250ml) chicken stock
2 teaspoons finely chopped fresh tarragon leaves
2 tablespoons cream
1 sheet frozen puff pastry, thawed

Cook chicken in large heated oiled pan, in batches, until browned all over. Heat butter in same pan; cook asparagus, leek and carrot, stirring, until leek is soft. Add flour; cook, stirring, until mixture thickens and bubbles. Gradually stir in stock; cook, stirring, until mixture boils and thickens. Return chicken to pan. [can be prepared ahead to this point; refrigerate overnight or freeze]

Stir tarragon and cream into chicken mixture. Bring to boil; simmer about 15 minutes or until chicken is tender.

Meanwhile, cut 4 x 10cm circles from pastry sheet; place circles on lightly oiled oven tray. Bake in very hot oven about 10 minutes or until browned. Place pastry circles over chicken and vegetables.

SERVES 4

Above Chicken and vegetables in tarragon cream
Right Thai fish balls

EGGPLANT ROLLS

1 large (350g) red capsicum
1 large (350g) yellow capsicum
2 large (1kg) eggplants, finely
   sliced lengthways
4 medium (480g) zucchini, sliced
1/4 cup (60ml) olive oil
1/4 cup (35g) sun-dried tomatoes in
   oil, drained, chopped
400g artichoke hearts,
   drained, chopped
125g fetta cheese, crumbled
2 tablespoons olive oil, extra
1 tablespoon balsamic vinegar

Quarter capsicums; remove and discard seeds and membranes. Place on oven trays, skin-side up, with eggplant and zucchini slices. Brush both sides of vegetables with oil; bake, uncovered, in hot oven about 5 minutes or until browned. Turn eggplant and zucchini; bake 5 minutes or until browned and softened. Drain.

Chop cooled zucchini and capsicum finely; combine in small bowl with the sun-dried tomato, artichoke and fetta. Divide vegetable mixture equally among eggplant slices; roll carefully, then place seam-side down, in shallow baking dish. [can be prepared ahead to this point; refrigerate overnight or freeze]

Drizzle half the combined extra oil and vinegar over rolls; bake, covered, about 15 minutes or until heated through. Drizzle rolls with remaining combined extra oil and vinegar.

SERVES 4

Opposite Salmon and dill coulibiac
Below Eggplant rolls

AROMATIC SPICED CHICKEN AND RICE

4 (880g) chicken thighs
4 (600g) chicken drumsticks
1/2 cup (125ml) lemon juice
1 tablespoon ground cumin
2 teaspoons ground coriander
1 tablespoon ghee
1 1/2 cups (300g) white
    long-grain rice
1 3/4 cups (430ml) chicken stock

2/3 cup (90g) slivered
    almonds, toasted
1/2 cup (75g) dried currants
1/2 cup finely chopped fresh
    coriander leaves

Place chicken in large pan of boiling water; simmer, covered, until just cooked. Drain chicken; place in large freezer-safe container, stir in juice and half the spices. Marinate chicken, covered, in refrigerator 3 hours. [can be prepared ahead to this point; refrigerate overnight or freeze]

Melt ghee in medium pan; cook rice and remaining spices, stirring, until rice is coated in ghee and spices are fragrant. Add stock. Bring to boil; simmer, covered tightly, about 12 minutes or until rice is just tender. Remove rice from heat; stand, covered, 5 minutes; stir in the almonds, currants and coriander.

Meanwhile, cook drained chicken pieces in large heated oiled pan until browned both sides and cooked through; serve with spiced rice.

SERVES 4

Plate from Gempo; fork from Home & Garden on the Mall; corkscrew from House in Newtown

Chopping board from Bayleak Leisure Store; tea-towel from Home & Garden on the Mall; baking dish from Accoutrement

BAKED CHICKEN, KUMARA AND SPINACH

250g fetta cheese
250g packet frozen spinach, thawed
2 large (1kg) kumara, sliced thinly
4 (680g) single chicken breast fillets, sliced thinly
1 large (200g) onion, chopped finely
2 teaspoons finely chopped fresh thyme
1/4 cup (60ml) light sour cream
1/2 cup (125ml) chicken stock
2 teaspoons plain flour
1 tablespoon water
2 cups (250g) grated pizza cheese

Crumble fetta into medium bowl. Using hands, squeeze excess moisture from spinach; mix spinach with fetta.

Boil, steam or microwave kumara until just tender; drain.

Meanwhile, cook chicken, in batches, in medium heated oiled pan until just cooked through and browned all over.

Cook onion and thyme in same pan, stirring, until onion is soft; stir into fetta mixture. Cook cream, stock and blended flour and water in same pan, stirring, until mixture boils and thickens.

Place half the kumara, half the chicken and all of the fetta mixture, in layers, in oiled 3-litre (12-cup) ovenproof dish. Repeat layering with remaining kumara and chicken; pour cream mixture over the top. [can be prepared ahead to this point; refrigerate overnight or freeze] Sprinkle with pizza cheese; bake, uncovered, in moderately hot oven about 30 minutes or until cheese melts and is browned lightly.

SERVES 4

Opposite Aromatic spiced chicken and rice
Above Baked chicken, kumara and spinach

Baking dish from Gempo; glass from House In Newtown

ALMOND, CHICKPEA AND PUMPKIN STEW

900g butternut pumpkin, chopped
1 large (500g) leek, sliced
575g bottled tomato pasta sauce
1 cup (250ml) water
425g can chickpeas, drained
1 tablespoon lemon juice
1 tablespoon ground cumin
1/2 cup (70g) slivered
almonds, toasted
200ml yogurt
2 tablespoons finely chopped
fresh mint leaves

Cook pumpkin and leek in large heated oiled pan, stirring, until leek is soft. Stir in the sauce, water, chickpeas, juice and cumin. Bring to boil; simmer, uncovered, about 20 minutes or until pumpkin is tender, stirring occasionally. [can be prepared ahead to this point; refrigerate overnight or freeze] Stir in almonds; serve with combined yogurt and mint.

SERVES 4

Above Almond, chickpea and pumpkin stew
Right Polenta wedges with ratatouille

POLENTA WEDGES WITH RATATOUILLE

3 cups (750ml) vegetable stock
1 cup (250ml) water
1 cup (170g) polenta
1/2 cup (40g) coarsely grated romano cheese
1/4 cup (60ml) olive oil
1 large (200g) onion, sliced
2 medium (400g) red capsicums
3 medium (360g) zucchini
400g can tomatoes
1/4 cup (60ml) tomato paste
2 tablespoons bottled pesto

Oil 22cm round sandwich cake pan.

Bring stock and water to boil in large pan; add polenta, simmer, stirring, about 10 minutes or until polenta thickens. Stir in cheese. Press polenta into prepared pan; cover, refrigerate 30 minutes or until set. [can be prepared ahead to this point; refrigerate overnight or freeze]

Heat 1 tablespoon of the oil in large pan; cook onion, stirring, until just soft. Halve and remove seeds from capsicums; cut the capsicum and zucchini into long, 1cm-wide strips; add to pan with the undrained crushed tomatoes, paste and pesto. Bring to boil; simmer, uncovered, until vegetables are tender.

Meanwhile, turn polenta onto board; cut into 8 wedges. Heat remaining oil in pan; cook polenta wedges, in batches, until browned both sides. Serve polenta wedges with ratatouille.

SERVES 4

SHELLS WITH SMOKED HAM IN MUSTARD-CHEESE SAUCE

500g shell pasta
60g butter
1/4 cup (35g) plain flour
1 litre (4 cups) milk
1 cup (125g) grated cheddar cheese
2 teaspoons seeded mustard
200g double-smoked ham, chopped
1 1/2 cups (210g) frozen corn kernels, thawed
6 green onions, chopped
3 cups (375g) grated pizza cheese

Cook pasta in large pan of boiling water, uncovered, until just tender; drain.

Heat butter in large pan, add flour; cook, stirring, until flour thickens and bubbles. Remove from heat; gradually stir in 3 cups of the milk (if recipe is to be frozen, add the remaining cup of milk). Cook, stirring, until mixture boils and thickens; stir in cheddar cheese, mustard, ham, corn and onion.

Gently stir pasta into pan with sauce; spoon into 2 1/2-litre (10-cup) lightly oiled baking dish. [can be prepared ahead to this point; refrigerate overnight or freeze] Sprinkle with pizza cheese; bake, uncovered, in moderately hot oven about 20 minutes or until top is browned.

SERVES 4 TO 6

Black dish from Accoutrement; glasses and placemat from Shack Homewares

MOROCCAN LEMON CHICKEN

2 tablespoons olive oil
1.5kg chicken pieces
1 large (200g) onion, sliced
2 cloves garlic, crushed
2 cinnamon sticks
2 teaspoons ground cumin
2 teaspoons ground turmeric
2 x 6cm strips lemon rind
1/3 cup (80ml) lemon juice

400g can tomatoes
¹/₂ cup (125ml) water
¹/₂ cup (60g) seeded black olives

Heat oil in large pan; cook chicken, in batches, until browned all over. Drain; cover to keep warm.

Add onion, garlic, cinnamon and ground spices to same pan; cook, stirring, until onion is soft. Return chicken to pan with rind, juice, undrained crushed tomatoes and water. Bring to boil; simmer, covered, about 40 minutes or until chicken is cooked through. [can be prepared ahead to this point; refrigerate up to 2 days or freeze]

Stir in olives; simmer, uncovered, about 10 minutes or until sauce thickens slightly. Discard cinnamon sticks.

SERVES 4

Opposite Shells with smoked ham in mustard-cheese sauce
Above Moroccan lemon chicken

SEAFOOD CASSEROLE

2 tablespoons olive oil
1 large (200g) onion, chopped
2 cloves garlic, crushed
400g can tomatoes
¼ cup (60ml) dry red wine
¼ cup (60ml) tomato paste
1 tablespoon brown sugar
1 tablespoon balsamic vinegar
½ cup (125ml) water
1kg marinara seafood mix
**2 tablespoons coarsely chopped
fresh oregano**

Heat oil in large pan; cook onion and garlic, stirring, until onion is soft. Add undrained crushed tomatoes, wine, paste, sugar, vinegar and water. Bring to boil; simmer, uncovered, about 20 minutes or until sauce thickens. [can be prepared ahead to this point; refrigerate for up to 2 days or freeze]

Add marinara mix to tomato sauce; simmer, uncovered, about 10 minutes or until seafood is cooked through. Stir in oregano just before serving.

SERVES 4

BEEF SKEWERS IN PEANUT AND CHILLI SAUCE

½ cup (125ml) peanut oil
**¼ cup (35g) raw unsalted peanuts,
toasted, chopped**
1 tablespoon honey
1 teaspoon sesame oil
2 tablespoons sweet chilli sauce
1 tablespoon lime juice
**1kg whole piece beef rump steak,
sliced thinly**
2 tablespoons water
1 medium (120g) carrot
2 medium (240g) zucchini

Blend or process peanut oil, peanuts, honey, sesame oil, sauce and juice until smooth. Thread beef onto 12 skewers; place skewers, in single layer, in shallow dish. Pour peanut sauce over skewers; cover, refrigerate 3 hours or overnight. [can be prepared ahead to this point; refrigerate for up to 2 days or freeze]

Drain skewers; place peanut sauce in small pan with water. Bring to boil; simmer, stirring, until sauce thickens slightly.

Using a vegetable peeler, cut carrot and zucchini into long, thin ribbons.

Cook skewers on heated oiled griddle (or grill or barbecue), in batches, until browned all over and cooked as desired. Serve drizzled with heated peanut sauce, and carrot and zucchini ribbons.

SERVES 4

Below Seafood casserole
Right above Beef skewers in peanut and chilli sauce
Right below Veal cutlets with lemon mustard butter

Plate from Sirocco Homewares; tray from Intarsia Homeware

VEAL CUTLETS WITH LEMON MUSTARD BUTTER

1/4 cup (60ml) lemon juice
2 tablespoons olive oil
1 tablespoon balsamic vinegar
2 cloves garlic, crushed
4 veal cutlets

LEMON MUSTARD BUTTER
125g butter
1 tablespoon seeded mustard
**1 tablespoon chopped
   sun-dried tomatoes**
**1 tablespoon chopped fresh
   flat-leaf parsley**
1 teaspoon grated lemon rind

Combine juice, oil, vinegar and garlic in large bowl. Add cutlets; coat with lemon mixture. Cover; refrigerate 3 hours or overnight. [can be prepared ahead to this point and frozen]

Drain cutlets; reserve lemon mixture. Cook cutlets on heated oiled griddle (or grill or barbecue) until browned both sides and cooked as desired, brushing occasionally with lemon mixture. Serve with sliced Lemon Mustard Butter.

Lemon Mustard Butter Combine all ingredients in small bowl. Place on baking paper; roll into log shape. Wrap log in plastic. [can be prepared ahead to this point; refrigerate overnight or freeze]

SERVES 4

Plates and glass from House In Newtown

MACARONI CHEESE WITH PESTO AND VEGETABLES

We used the traditional basil pesto but try experimenting with others if you like. We also used a small elbow macaroni in this recipe but, again, experiment with any short pasta — like penne or fusilli.

1 medium (200g) red capsicum
250g elbow macaroni
1/2 cup (125ml) bottled pesto
5 (190g) pattipan squash, quartered
2 tablespoons finely chopped fresh basil leaves
1 cup (80g) coarsely grated parmesan cheese
1/4 cup (80g) pine nuts, toasted
8 slices prosciutto, chopped
300ml cream
1 cup (100g) coarsely grated mozzarella cheese

Quarter capsicum, remove seeds and membranes. Roast under grill or in very hot oven, skin-side up, until skin blisters and blackens. Cover capsicum pieces in plastic or paper for 5 minutes; peel away skin. Slice capsicum thinly.

Cook pasta in large pan of boiling water, uncovered, until just tender; drain. Combine pesto, squash, basil, parmesan, half the pine nuts and half the prosciutto in large bowl; gently toss with capsicum and pasta. [can be prepared ahead to this point; refrigerate overnight or freeze]

Stir in cream. Place pasta mixture in oiled 6-cup (1.5-litre) ovenproof dish; sprinkle with combined mozzarella, remaining prosciutto and remaining chopped pine nuts. Bake, uncovered, in moderate oven about 25 minutes or until heated through and browned lightly.

SERVES 4

Plates from Pillivuyt, cutlery from Home & Garden on the Mall

Left Macaroni cheese with pesto and vegetables
Right Felafel with tangy garlic sauce

FELAFEL WITH TANGY GARLIC SAUCE

We used packaged felafel mix for this recipe, available from Middle-Eastern food shops and many health food stores.

1½ cups felafel mix
⅓ cup (55g) burghul
½ cup finely chopped fresh flat-leaf parsley
1 tablespoon ground coriander
1¼ cups (310ml) water
vegetable oil, for deep-frying
⅓ cup (80ml) water, extra
⅓ cup (80ml) tahini
⅓ cup (80ml) lemon juice
2 cloves garlic, crushed

Combine felafel mix, burghul, parsley, coriander and all the water in large bowl; refrigerate, covered, for about 2 hours or until all liquid is absorbed and mixture holds together. [can be prepared ahead to this point; refrigerate overnight or freeze]

Shape level tablespoons of mixture into patties. Heat oil in large pan; deep-fry patties, in batches, until browned and cooked through. Drain.

Whisk together combined remaining ingredients in small bowl until smooth; drizzle over heated felafel.

SERVES 4 TO 6

Square plate and cup from House In Newtown

Grains and cereals

We've given basic cooking methods for rice, couscous and freekah. Each of the recipe suggestions will serve 4 with the quantities shown, as well as with similar amounts of any other of the wide range of cereal and grain products also available: farro, barley, millet, corn, quinoa, rye, oats and kasha.

STEAMED RICE

We have used white rice here but you can use brown rice and increase the cooking time according to the package directions. Combine 2 cups (400g) long- or short-grain white rice and 1 litre (4 cups) water in medium heavy-based pan; cover tightly, bring to boil, reduce heat as low as possible. Cook about 15 minutes or until water is absorbed and rice is tender; remove pan from heat. Stand, covered, for 10 minutes, fluff rice with a fork.

COUSCOUS

Couscous, originally from North Africa, is the fine-grain cereal made from semolina that is almost as common as rice today. Place 2 cups (400g) couscous in medium bowl; cover with 2 cups (500ml) boiling water. Stand about 2 minutes then add 40g melted butter; gently toss couscous, using a fork, to separate grains.

FREEKAH

Packaged in both cracked and wholegrain form, greenwheat freekah comes to us from the Middle-East. It is easy to prepare, versatile and as healthy as it is delicious. Place 1 cup (165g) freekah in large pan; cover with 4 cups cold water. Bring to boil; boil, uncovered, stirring occasionally, about 20 minutes or until freekah is just tender. At this stage, we suggest rinsing cooked freekah under hot water to separate the kernels; drain well before serving.

⊏ **DRIED FRUITS AND ALMONDS** Combine 1 quantity cooked cereal/grain with 1 1/4 cups (200g) toasted chopped almonds, 1 cup (150g) chopped dried apricots, 1/2 cup (80g) chopped dates, 1/2 cup (85g) raisins and 1 tablespoon chopped glace ginger in large bowl.

⊏ **TOMATO, LEMON THYME AND CHILLI SALSA** Combine 1 quantity cooked cereal/grain in large bowl with 2 large (500g) chopped tomatoes, 1 small (100g) chopped red onion, 3 small seeded and finely chopped red chillies, 2 tablespoons finely chopped fresh lemon thyme and 1/4 cup (60ml) each of olive oil and balsamic vinegar.

⊏ **TABOULLEH WITH A DIFFERENCE** Combine 1 quantity cooked cereal/grain in large bowl with 1 crushed clove garlic, 2 cups finely chopped fresh parsley, 1/4 cup finely chopped fresh mint leaves, 2 small (260g) finely chopped tomatoes, 1 small (100g) finely chopped red onion and 1/2 cup (125ml) each of olive oil and lemon juice.

⊏ **HERB AND GREEN ONION** Combine 1 quantity cooked cereal/grain in large bowl with 1 tablespoon French salad dressing, 2 tablespoons finely chopped fresh parsley and 1 tablespoon each finely chopped fresh basil leaves, fresh mint leaves and green onion.

⊏ **EGGPLANT AND PINE NUT** Combine 1 quantity cooked cereal/grain in large bowl with 2 tablespoons each of chopped char-grilled eggplant, toasted pine nuts and fresh coriander leaves.

⊏ **A TRIO OF MUSHROOMS AND LEMON GRASS** Heat 2 tablespoons peanut oil in medium pan; cook 100g each sliced enoki, shiitake and button mushrooms, 2 crushed cloves garlic, 1 tablespoon chopped fresh lemon grass and 1 small (100g) finely chopped red onion, stirring, until mushrooms are browned lightly and tender. Gently toss mushroom mixture in large bowl with 1 quantity cooked cereal/grain.

⊏ **ROASTED SPICED PUMPKIN** Combine 1/2 chopped butternut pumpkin, 3 teaspoons cumin seeds, 1/2 teaspoon ground cardamom and 1/4 cup (60ml) peanut oil in baking dish. Bake, uncovered, in very hot oven about 20 minutes or until pumpkin is tender. Combine pumpkin in large bowl with 1 quantity cooked cereal/grain and 1/4 cup (60ml) orange juice.

⊏ **SPICY LIME** Combine 1 quantity cooked cereal/grain in large bowl with 2 teaspoons toasted caraway seeds, 2 teaspoons ground cumin, 2 teaspoons ground turmeric, 1 teaspoon ground coriander and 2 teaspoons finely grated fresh lime rind.

⊏ **CHORIZO AND SUN-DRIED TOMATO** Combine 1 quantity cooked cereal/grain in large bowl with 2/3 cup (170g) chopped chorizo sausage, 1/3 cup (50g) drained and chopped sun-dried tomatoes in oil and 2 tablespoons each of finely chopped fresh basil leaves and coarsely grated parmesan cheese.

Clockwise from top centre: Herb and green onion couscous; Roasted spiced pumpkin and rice; Taboulleh with a difference; Spicy lime couscous; Dried fruits and almonds with rice; Eggplant and pine nuts with freekah

QUAIL FLORENTINE

2 bacon rashers, chopped finely
250g packet frozen spinach,
   thawed, drained
1 cup (200g) ricotta cheese
1 tablespoon finely chopped
   fresh sage leaves
8 quail
2 tablespoons olive oil
1 medium (200g) onion, chopped
2 cloves garlic, crushed
400g can tomato puree

Cook bacon, stirring, in small dry pan until crisp; drain on absorbent paper. Squeeze excess liquid from spinach; chop roughly. Combine bacon and spinach in medium bowl with ricotta and sage.

Remove and discard necks from quail. Rinse quail under cold water; pat dry. Fill quail with spinach mixture; secure with toothpicks, tie legs together, tuck wings under. [can be prepared ahead to this point; refrigerate overnight or freeze]

Heat half of the olive oil in small pan; cook onion and garlic, stirring, until onion is soft. Add puree; cook 2 minutes. Pour puree mixture into large baking dish. Add quail to dish; brush with remaining oil. Bake, uncovered, in very hot oven about 25 minutes or until cooked through.

SERVES 4

CURRIED FRIED RICE

1¹/₂ cups (300g) long-grain
   white rice
1 tablespoon vegetable oil
2 (340g) chicken breast
   fillets, chopped
1 medium (150g) onion, sliced
¹/₃ cup (80ml) mild curry paste
¹/₂ cup (125ml) coconut milk
¹/₂ cup (70g) slivered
   almonds, toasted
200ml yogurt
2 teaspoons finely chopped
   fresh mint leaves

Cook rice in large pan of boiling water, uncovered, until just tender; drain.

Meanwhile, heat oil in large pan; cook chicken, in batches, until browned all over. Add onion and paste to same pan; cook, stirring, until onion is soft. Return chicken to pan; add rice, stir until heated through. [can be prepared ahead to this point; refrigerate overnight or freeze]

Stir in coconut milk and almonds; serve with combined yogurt and mint.

SERVES 4

Opposite Quail Florentine
Above Curried fried rice

Plate from Home & Garden on the Mall; bowl and canister from House In Newtown

MINTED LAMB SKEWERS

10 (800g) lamb fillets
1 tablespoon mild curry powder
1 tablespoon finely chopped
     fresh lemon grass
2 teaspoons finely grated
     fresh ginger
¹/₄ cup (60ml) peanut oil
¹/₂ cup finely chopped fresh
     mint leaves

1 tablespoon fish sauce
4 cloves garlic, crushed
1 cup (150g) pistachios,
     chopped finely

Cut lamb into 2cm cubes. Combine curry powder, lemon grass, ginger, oil, mint, sauce and garlic in large bowl; add lamb, coat with spice mixture. Thread lamb onto 12 skewers.

Place skewers in shallow dish. Cover; refrigerate 3 hours or overnight. [can be

prepared ahead to this point; refrigerate for up to 2 days or freeze]

Place nuts on tray; roll skewers in nuts until coated evenly. Cook skewers on heated oiled griddle (or grill or barbecue) until golden brown and cooked through.

SERVES 4

Above Minted lamb skewers
Right above Ricotta and spinach lasagne
Right Old-fashioned crumbed chicken and mash

RICOTTA AND SPINACH LASAGNE

1kg spinach, trimmed
3 eggs, beaten lightly
2 cups (400g) ricotta cheese
1/4 cup (20g) coarsely grated
  parmesan cheese
3 green onions, chopped
1 1/2 cups (375ml) bottled tomato
  pasta sauce
12 sheets instant lasagne
1 cup (120g) coarsely grated
  cheddar cheese

Boil, steam or microwave spinach until just wilted; drain. Squeeze excess liquid from spinach; chop roughly. Combine eggs, ricotta, parmesan and onions in large bowl; stir in spinach.

Spread half of the pasta sauce over base of oiled shallow baking dish; cover with 3 sheets lasagne, top with a third of the spinach mixture. Cover spinach layer with 3 sheets lasagne; repeat layering with remaining spinach mixture and remaining lasagne sheets. Top lasagne with remaining tomato sauce; sprinkle with cheddar cheese.

Cover lasagne with foil; bake in moderate oven 40 minutes. [can be prepared ahead to this point; refrigerate for up to 2 days or freeze]

Remove foil; bake 20 minutes or until browned on top.

SERVES 4

Place setting from Accoutrement

OLD-FASHIONED CRUMBED CHICKEN AND MASH

4 (680g) chicken breast fillets
plain flour
1 egg, beaten lightly
1 cup (70g) stale breadcrumbs
2 teaspoons ground cumin
2 teaspoons sweet paprika
1/4 cup (35g) sesame seeds
5 medium (1kg) potatoes, chopped
1 clove garlic, crushed
60g butter

Coat chicken in flour; dip in egg then combined breadcrumbs, cumin, paprika and seeds. Place chicken, in single layer, on tray; cover, refrigerate 30 minutes. [can be prepared ahead to this point; refrigerate overnight or freeze]

Cook chicken in large heated oiled pan until cooked through.

Meanwhile, boil, steam or microwave potatoes until tender; drain. Mash potatoes with garlic and butter. Serve potato mash with chicken.

SERVES 4

Plates from The Design Store; placemat from Shack Homewares; tiles from Country Floors

BEEF AND PASTA COUNTRY CASSEROLE

750g whole piece beef chuck steak
2 tablespoons olive oil
5 small (400g) onions, quartered
2 cloves garlic, crushed
2 medium (240g) carrots, chopped
1 cup (250ml) dry red wine
3 cups (750ml) beef stock
1/2 cup (125ml) tomato paste
2 cups (180g) spiral pasta
3 medium (360g) zucchini, sliced thickly

Cut beef into 3cm cubes. Heat half the oil in large pan; cook beef, in batches, until browned all over and cooked as desired.

Heat remaining oil in same pan; cook onion and garlic, stirring, until onion is soft. Return beef to pan with carrot, wine, stock and paste. Bring to boil; simmer, covered, about 1 hour or until beef is tender. [can be prepared ahead to this point; refrigerate for up to 2 days or freeze]

Cook pasta in large pan of boiling water, uncovered, until just tender; drain. Add zucchini to pan with beef mixture. Bring to boil; simmer about 10 minutes or until zucchini is just tender. Add pasta; stir until heated through.

SERVES 4

Below Beef and pasta country casserole
Right Baked semolina with tomato and olive sauce

BAKED SEMOLINA WITH TOMATO AND OLIVE SAUCE

2 cups (500ml) vegetable stock
2 cups (500ml) milk
1 cup (160g) semolina
1 egg, beaten
1 cup (125g) coarsely grated
    cheddar cheese
1 cup (80g) coarsely grated
    parmesan cheese
3 cups (750ml) bottled tomato and
    basil pasta sauce

1/3 cup (40g) seeded black
    olives, sliced
2 tablespoons finely chopped
    fresh oregano
2 teaspoons sugar

Bring stock and milk to boil in large pan. Stir in semolina; cook, stirring, about 15 minutes or until mixture thickens. Stir in the egg, half of the cheddar and three-quarters of the parmesan; spread semolina evenly into oiled deep 19cm cake pan. Cover; refrigerate 2 hours or until firm. [can be prepared ahead to this point; refrigerate up to 3 days]

Turn semolina onto board; cut in half, cut each half into 1cm slices. Combine pasta sauce, olives, oregano and sugar in medium bowl; spoon half the tomato sauce mixture into oiled 12-cup (3-litre) ovenproof dish; top with overlapping slices of semolina. Drizzle remaining tomato sauce mixture over semolina; sprinkle with remaining cheddar and parmesan.

Bake, covered, in hot oven, 20 minutes. Remove cover; bake further 10 minutes or until browned lightly. Stand 10 minutes before serving.

SERVES 4

Potato panache

There are more than 30 varieties of potatoes available commercially today.
Some are better for mashing, others for roasting, yet others for making chips.
Experiment with different types until you find the one you like best.
On average, about 5 medium-size potatoes
is 1kg in weight.

Mashed potatoes

Chop 1kg potatoes roughly; cook in large pan of boiling water, uncovered, until tender. Drain then mash potato in large bowl with 20g butter and $^1/_4$ cup (60ml) milk; add salt and pepper to taste.

PUMPKIN Combine with $1^1/_4$ cups (500g) cooked pumpkin mashed with $^1/_4$ teaspoon ground nutmeg.

PESTO, PINE NUT & PARMESAN Combine with 2 tablespoons toasted pine nuts, 2 tablespoons bottled pesto and $^1/_2$ cup (40g) coarsely grated parmesan cheese.

ITALIAN Combine with 4 chopped, cooked and drained bacon rashers, 2 tablespoons finely chopped fresh chives and $^1/_3$ cup (80ml) Italian salad dressing.

CARAMELISED LEEKS Slice 2 leeks thinly; cook in medium heated oiled pan until browned. Add 2 tablespoons brown sugar; cook, stirring, until mixture caramelises. Stir leeks into mash. Reheat pan; cook pancetta until crisp, stir into mash.

Mashed potatoes and pumpkin

Pine nut, pesto and parmesan mash

Grated potatoes

Finely grate 500g peeled potatoes, squeeze out excess liquid. Pat dry with absorbent paper.

CAJUN Combine with 1 tablespoon plain flour and 2 teaspoons Cajun seasoning. Drop $^1/_4$ cups mixture into heated oiled pan; cook, in batches, until browned both sides and heated through.

PANCAKE Combine 2 cups (325g) powdered pancake and pikelet mix in large bowl with 2 beaten eggs, $1^1/_2$ cups (375ml) milk and 130g can creamed corn. Drop $^1/_4$ cups mixture into heated oiled pan; cook, in batches, until browned both sides and cooked through.

OMELETTE Heat 2 tablespoons olive oil in 21cm non-stick pan; cook 1 medium (150g) sliced onion until soft. Spread potatoes evenly over onion. Beat 6 eggs in large jug, pour over potatoes; cook until omelette is just set. Cook under grill until top is browned and mixture cooked through.

HASH BROWN Deep-fry grated potato, in $^1/_4$ cup batches, in hot oil until crisp; drain on absorbent paper. Sprinkle with $^1/_2$ teaspoon chicken salt.

Boiled potatoes

Halve 500g tiny new potatoes; cook in pan of boiling water until tender, drain.

FRENCH ONION Combine with 300ml sour cream, 40g packet French onion soup mix and 1 tablespoon chopped fresh parsley.

GREEK Combine with 250g tub tzatziki and 1 tablespoon finely chopped fresh mint leaves.

HERB Combine with 1/2 cup (125ml) French salad dressing and 1 tablespoon each finely chopped fresh parsley, fresh mint leaves and fresh chives.

MADRAS CURRY Heat 1 tablespoon peanut oil in large non-stick pan; cook 1 tablespoon Madras curry paste 1 minute. Stir in potatoes; coat with paste. Add 1/4 cup (30g) frozen peas; cook until just heated through. Drizzle with 1/4 cup (60ml) yogurt.

Madras curried
potato and peas

Potato wedges

Wedges and fries

FRENCH FRIES Slice 500g potatoes thinly; place in single layer on oven tray, sprinkle with 11/2 teaspoons garlic salt; spray with cooking oil. Cook, uncovered, in very hot oven 15 minutes, turn slices over; cook about 15 minutes or until browned and crisp.

WEDGES Cut 500g potatoes into thin wedges; place on oven tray, sprinkle with 1/2 teaspoon each ground cumin and ground coriander. Drizzle with 1 tablespoon olive oil; cook, uncovered, in very hot oven about 30 minutes or until wedges are browned.

CRINKLE-CUT Cut potatoes with crinkle cutter; place on oven tray with 2 sprigs fresh rosemary. Sprinkle with cracked black pepper to taste; cook, uncovered, in very hot oven about 30 minutes or until browned.

Cajun-spiced grated
potato cakes

Platter, dish and zester from Accoutrement

MARINATED
CHAR-GRILLED OCTOPUS

2kg baby octopus
1/2 cup (125ml) plum sauce
1/3 cup (80ml) barbecue sauce
1/3 cup (80ml) sweet chilli sauce
2 tablespoons tomato sauce
1/3 cup (80ml) lemon juice
1 tablespoon grated fresh ginger
3 cloves garlic, crushed
1/4 cup (60ml) peanut oil

Remove and discard heads and beaks from octopus; cut in half. Place octopus in medium bowl with the combined sauces, lemon juice, ginger, garlic and oil. Cover; refrigerate 3 hours or overnight. [can be prepared ahead to this point and frozen]

Drain octopus; discard marinade. Cook octopus on heated oiled griddle (or grill or barbecue), in batches, until browned and tender.

SERVES 4

BRAISED SPATCHCOCK WITH
CHOY SUM AND POTATOES

4 x 500g spatchcock
2 teaspoons grated lime rind
1/4 cup (60ml) lime juice
2 teaspoons sweet chilli sauce
3 cloves garlic, crushed
12 (480g) tiny new potatoes, unpeeled, halved
2 tablespoons peanut oil
600g choy sum, chopped
2 tablespoons lime juice, extra
1 tablespoon finely chopped fresh coriander leaves

Cut along both sides of spatchcock backbones; discard backbones. Cut along breast bones, dividing spatchcock in half.

Place the spatchcock in large pan of boiling water; simmer, uncovered, about 10 minutes or until just cooked. Remove spatchcock from pan; place, in single layer, in shallow dish. Discard cooking liquid.

Meanwhile, combine rind, juice, sauce and garlic in small jug; pour over spatch-cock. Cover; refrigerate 3 hours. [can be prepared ahead to this point; refrigerate overnight or freeze]

Drain spatchcock; reserve marinade. Cook spatchcock, in batches, in large heated oiled pan until browned all over and cooked through, brushing with reserved marinade occasionally. Cover to keep warm.

Meanwhile, boil, steam or microwave potatoes until just tender; drain. Heat 1 tablespoon of the oil in medium pan; add potato until browned and tender. Add choy sum; cook, stirring, until just wilted.

Drizzle spatchcock with combined remaining oil, extra juice and coriander; serve with potato and choy sum mixture.

SERVES 4

Above Marinated char-grilled octopus
Right above Meatballs with chilli mushroom sauce
Right Braised spatchcock with choy sum and potatoes

MEATBALLS WITH CHILLI MUSHROOM SAUCE

500g pork and veal mince
1 cup (70g) stale breadcrumbs
**1/4 cup finely chopped
   fresh oregano**
3 cloves garlic, crushed
1/3 cup (80ml) tomato paste
1 egg, beaten
1 tablespoon olive oil
250g button mushrooms, sliced
2 x 400g cans tomatoes
1/4 cup (60ml) mild chilli sauce

Combine mince, breadcrumbs, oregano, garlic, paste and egg in medium bowl; roll level tablespoons of mixture into balls. Place meatballs on oiled oven tray; bake, uncovered, in moderately hot oven about 15 minutes or until cooked through.

Meanwhile, heat oil in large pan; cook mushrooms, stirring, until just soft. Add undrained crushed tomatoes and sauce to pan. Bring to boil; simmer, uncovered, 5 minutes. Add meatballs; cook, stirring, 2 minutes. [can be prepared ahead to this point; refrigerate overnight or freeze]

SERVES 4

Bowls, tureen and plate from The Bay Tree Kitchen Shop

ROSEMARY-CRUMBED LAMB CUTLETS

12 lamb cutlets, trimmed
2 tablespoons plain flour
1 egg, beaten
1/2 teaspoon mustard powder
1/3 cup (35g) cornflake crumbs
1 teaspoon finely chopped
  fresh rosemary
1/2 teaspoon cracked black pepper
1/4 cup (60ml) port
1/2 cup (125ml) redcurrant jelly
2 tablespoons seeded mustard

Coat cutlets with flour. Dip cutlets in combined egg and mustard powder; press on combined crumbs, rosemary and pepper. [can be prepared ahead to this point; refrigerate overnight or freeze]

Cook cutlets, uncovered, in large heated oiled pan until browned lightly and cooked through; drain on absorbent paper.

Meanwhile, cook port, jelly and mustard, stirring, in small pan until heated through; serve with cutlets.

SERVES 4

Plates, salt and pepper mills, mat and strainer from Accoutrement

BAKED CREAMY FETTUCCINE WITH BEEF

1 tablespoon olive oil
500g minced beef
2 cups (500ml) bottled tomato
   pasta sauce
1 cup (250ml) water
375g fettuccine
200g butter
3/4 cup (110g) plain flour
1 litre (4 cups) milk
1 3/4 cups (220g) coarsely grated
   cheddar cheese
2 cups (140g) stale breadcrumbs
2 tablespoons finely chopped
   fresh parsley

Heat oil in large pan; cook beef, stirring, until browned all over. Add pasta sauce and water; simmer, uncovered, about 15 minutes or until beef mixture thickens.

Meanwhile, cook pasta in large pan of boiling water, uncovered, until just tender; drain.

Heat 150g of the butter in medium pan. Add flour; cook, stirring, until mixture thickens and bubbles. Remove from heat; gradually stir in milk. Return to heat; stir until white sauce boils and thickens. Remove from heat; stir in 3/4 cup of the cheddar cheese.

Combine remaining melted butter with breadcrumbs, parsley and remaining cheddar cheese in medium bowl.

Combine pasta with white sauce in shallow 2.5-litre (10-cup) ovenproof dish; top with mince mixture then sprinkle over breadcrumb mixture. [can be prepared ahead to this point; refrigerate overnight or freeze]

Bake, uncovered, in moderately hot oven about 30 minutes or until browned lightly and heated through.

SERVES 4 TO 6

PORK, KUMARA AND LENTIL CURRY

750g whole piece pork neck
2 medium (300g) onions, sliced
1/4 cup (60ml) mild curry paste
2 x 400g cans tomatoes
1 large (500g) kumara, chopped
1/2 cup (100g) red lentils
1 cup (250ml) coconut milk
500g spinach, trimmed
1 tablespoon finely chopped fresh
   coriander leaves

Cut pork into 2cm cubes; cook in large heated oiled pan, in batches, until well browned. Add onion and paste to same pan; cook, uncovered, until onion is soft.

Return pork to pan; stir in undrained crushed tomatoes. Bring to boil; simmer, covered, for 1 1/4 hours. [can be prepared ahead to this point; refrigerate overnight or freeze]

Meanwhile, cook kumara, uncovered, in medium heated oiled pan until just browned; add to pan with pork mixture, stir in lentils. Bring to boil; simmer, uncovered, about 15 minutes or until kumara and lentils are tender and pork is cooked through, stirring occasionally.

Stir in milk, spinach and coriander; cook, stirring until spinach is just wilted.

SERVES 4

Above Baked creamy fettuccine with beef
Opposite above Rosemary-crumbed
lamb cutlets
Opposite below Pork, kumara and lentil curry

COMBINATION FRIED RICE

1½ cups (300g) long-grain
    white rice
200g pork sausages
2 tablespoons peanut oil
2 eggs, beaten lightly
250g baby corn, sliced
1 medium (200g) red capsicum,
    sliced thinly
1 cup (80g) bean sprouts
6 green onions, chopped
1 tablespoon soy sauce
1 tablespoon oyster sauce

Cook rice in large pan of boiling water, uncovered, until just tender; drain well.

Meanwhile, cook sausages, uncovered, in large heated oiled pan until cooked through; drain on absorbent paper. Cut sausages into slices; combine with rice in large bowl. [can be prepared ahead to this point; refrigerate overnight or freeze]

Heat 1 teaspoon of the oil in wok or large pan; cook egg, tilting pan, over medium heat until omelette is almost set. Roll omelette; cut into thin strips.

Heat remaining oil in same pan; stir-fry corn, capsicum, sprouts and onion until vegetables are just tender. Add rice mixture, omelette and combined sauces; stir-fry until heated through.
SERVES 4

PEPPER-CRUSTED FISH WITH RED CAPSICUM CREAM

We used blue eye, a subtly flavoured, firm white fish but you can substitute it with fish fillets of your choice.

1 tablespoon polenta
1 tablespoon plain flour
1 tablespoon ground cumin
1 tablespoon cracked black pepper
4 (800g) white fish fillets
¼ cup (60ml) olive oil

RED CAPSICUM CREAM
3 small (450g) red capsicums
2 cloves garlic, crushed
½ cup (125ml) cream
1 tablespoon chopped fresh chives

Combine polenta, flour, cumin and pepper in medium bowl. Brush fish with water; toss in polenta mixture to coat.

Heat oil in large non-stick pan; cook fish, in batches, until browned lightly both sides and cooked through. Drain fish on absorbent paper. Serve with Red Capsicum Cream.

Red Capsicum Cream Quarter capsicums; remove seeds and membranes. Grill capsicum, skin-side up, until skin blisters and blackens. Cover capsicum pieces in plastic or paper for 5 minutes; peel away skin. Blend or process capsicum with garlic until smooth. [can be prepared ahead to this point; refrigerate overnight or freeze]

Place capsicum mixture in small pan; bring to boil. Add cream and chives; stir over medium heat until heated through.

SERVES 4

Opposite Combination fried rice
Below Pepper-crusted fish with red capsicum cream

LAMB SHANKS WITH BARLEY IN RED WINE

**8 (1.5kg) French-trimmed
lamb shanks
2 medium (300g) onions
3 cloves garlic, crushed
4 medium (480g) carrots, chopped
1/2 cup (65g) pearl barley, rinsed
1 cup (250ml) dry red wine
1 cup (250ml) beef stock
425g can tomatoes
1/4 cup (60ml) tomato paste
1 tablespoon finely chopped fresh
thyme leaves**

Cook lamb, in batches, in large heated oiled pan until browned lightly. Halve onions lengthways; cut into thick wedges. Add onion and garlic to same pan; cook, stirring, until onion is soft.

Return lamb to pan; add carrots, barley, wine, stock, undrained crushed tomatoes and paste. Bring to boil; simmer, covered, 1³/4 hours, stirring occasionally. [can be prepared ahead to this point; refrigerate overnight or freeze]

Stir in thyme; simmer, uncovered, about 15 minutes or until lamb is tender.

SERVES 4

MEXICALI BEAN AND RICE PIE

**2 cups (400g) calrose rice
1¹/4 cups (310ml) water
1¹/2 cups (375ml) beef stock
1 egg, beaten
2 cups (250g) coarsely grated
cheddar cheese
450g can refried beans
1¹/2 cups (375ml) bottled tomato
pasta sauce
1 medium (190g) tomato, chopped
6 green onions, sliced
2/3 cup (160ml) sour cream**

Oil 34cm pizza pan. Place rice, water and stock in large pan. Bring to boil; simmer tightly, covered, about 15 minutes or until rice is tender and liquid absorbed. Transfer rice to large bowl; when cool, stir in egg and half the cheddar cheese.

Using wet hands, press rice mixture evenly into prepared pan; bake, uncovered, in moderate oven about 40 minutes or until browned lightly. [can be prepared ahead to this point; refrigerate overnight or freeze]

Place beans in medium bowl; stir until smooth. Spread rice base with sauce; sprinkle with half of the remaining cheese. Spread with beans; sprinkle with half of the combined tomato and onion, then the remaining cheese. Bake, uncovered, in hot oven about 20 minutes or until cheese melts and pie is heated through. Top with sour cream and remaining tomato and onion.

SERVES 4

CHILLI, CHUTNEY AND COCONUT PORK

750g pork strips
1 cup (350g) mango chutney
2 fresh small red chillies,
   seeded, chopped
1 tablespoon ground cumin
2 cloves garlic, crushed
2 teaspoons finely grated
   fresh ginger
2 tablespoons lemon juice
1 large (350g) red capsicum, sliced
1 cup (250ml) coconut milk
1/2 cup coarsely chopped fresh
   coriander leaves

Combine pork, chutney, chilli, cumin, garlic, ginger and juice in large bowl. Cover; refrigerate 3 hours or overnight. [can be prepared ahead to this point; refrigerate overnight or freeze]

Cook capsicum in heated oiled wok or large pan, stirring, until almost soft; remove from pan.

Stir-fry pork mixture, in batches, in same pan until cooked through. Add capsicum and milk; cook, stirring, about 1 minute or until heated through. Just before serving, stir in coriander.

SERVES 4

Opposite above   Lamb shanks with barley in red wine
Opposite below   Mexicali bean and rice pie
Below   Chilli, chutney and coconut pork

GLOSSARY

chorizo

pepperoni

csabai

prosciutto

BACON RASHERS also known as slices of bacon; made from pork side, cured and smoked.

BARBECUE SAUCE a spicy, tomato-based sauce used to marinate, baste or as an accompaniment.

BARLEY a nutritious grain used in soups and stews as well as in whisky- and beer-making.
Pearl barley has had the husk discarded and been steamed and polished (like rice).

BREADCRUMBS
Packaged fine-textured, crunchy, purchased crumbs.
Stale 1- or 2-day-old bread made into crumbs by grating, blending or processing.

BRUSCHETTA Correctly pronounced *broo skeh tah*, this Italian snack is bread rubbed with garlic-infused olive oil, toasted and served with various different toppings.

BURGHUL also known as bulghur wheat; hulled steamed wheat kernels that, once dried, are crushed into various size grains. Used in Middle-Eastern dishes such as kibbeh and taboulleh.

BUTTER salted or unsalted ("sweet") butter; 125g is equal to 1 stick butter.

BUTTERMILK low-fat milk cultured with bacteria to give it a slightly sour, tangy taste; substitute low-fat yogurt.

CAJUN SEASONING a blend of paprika, basil, onion, fennel, thyme, cayenne and white pepper; used in the Deep South (USA) style of cooking.

CAPERS the grey-green buds of a warm-climate (usually Mediterranean) shrub sold either dried and salted, or pickled in a vinegar brine; their piquancy enhances sauces and dressings.

CHEESE
Fetta Greek in origin; a crumbly textured goat or sheep milk cheese having a sharp, salty taste.
Haloumi a firm, cream-coloured sheep milk cheese matured in brine; somewhat like a minty, salty fetta in flavour, haloumi can be grilled or fried, briefly, without breaking down.
Mozzarella a semi-soft cheese with a delicate, fresh taste; has a low melting point and stringy texture when heated.
Parmesan a sharp-tasting, dry, hard cheese, made from skim or part-skim milk and aged for at least a year before being sold.
Pizza cheese a commercial blend of varying proportions of processed grated cheddar, mozzarella and parmesan.
Ricotta a sweet, fairly moist, fresh curd cheese having a low fat content.
Romano a hard, straw-coloured cheese with a grainy texture and sharp, tangy flavour, made from either cow and goat or sheep milk; good for grating.

CHICKEN
Breast fillet breast halved, skinned and boned.
Maryland leg and thigh still connected in a single piece; bones and skin intact.
Tenderloin thin strip of meat lying just under the breast.
Thigh cutlet thigh with skin and centre bone intact; also known as a chicken chop.
Thigh fillet thigh with skin and centre bone removed.

CHILLI SAUCE our recipes use a hot Chinese variety made of chillies, salt and vinegar; use sparingly, increasing amounts to taste. **Sweet Chilli Sauce** is a fairly mild, Thai-type sauce made from red chillies, sugar, garlic and vinegar.

COCONUT MILK pure, unsweetened coconut milk available in cans.

CORNFLOUR thickening agent also known as cornstarch.

COUSCOUS a fine, grain-like cereal product, originally from North Africa, made from semolina rolled into balls.

CREAM
Fresh (minimum fat content 35%) also known as pure cream and pouring cream; has no additives like commercially thickened cream.
Light (minimum fat content 18%) also known as single cream. Doesn't hold a shape but is pourable.
Light sour (minimum fat content 18%) cream specifically cultured to produce its characteristic tart flavour; thinner than normal sour cream so should not be substituted in cooking because the consistency will affect recipe results.
Reduced (minimum fat content 25%) not suitable for whipping but good in sauces, soups and desserts as a lower-fat alternative to full cream.
Sour (minimum fat content 35%) a thick, commercially cultured soured cream good for dips, toppings and desserts such as baked cheesecakes.

CREME FRAICHE (minimum fat content 35%; not low in fat as many believe) velvety texture and tangy taste; available in cartons from delicatessens and supermarkets. To make creme fraiche, combine 300ml cream with 300ml sour cream in bowl, cover, stand at room temperature until mixture is thick; this will take 1 or 2 days, depending on room temperature. Refrigerate before using. Makes about 2$\frac{1}{2}$ cups (625ml).

haloumi

romano

parmesan

ricotta

mozzarella

grated mozzarella

fetta

pizza cheese

CURRY PASTE
Green commercial versions consist of red onion, green chilli, soy bean oil, garlic, galangal, lemon grass, shrimp paste, citrus peel and coriander seeds.
Madras commercial versions consist of coriander, cumin, pepper, turmeric, chilli, garlic, ginger, vinegar and oil.
Red commercial versions consist of red chilli, onion, garlic, soy bean oil, lemon rind, shrimp paste, cumin, paprika, turmeric and pepper.

DAMPER originally, unleavened bread cooked in the ashen coals of a campfire; today, available commercially in loaf and mini sizes enriched with butter and milk.

EGGPLANT also known as aubergine.

FELAFEL MIX also spelled falafel; a packaged dry mixture of chickpeas, broad (fava) beans, oat flakes, parsley and herbs used for

convenience, replacing the labour-intensive but delicious homemade patty eaten throughout the Middle East and North Africa.

FILLO PASTRY also known as phyllo; tissue-thin pastry sheets purchased chilled or frozen that are easy to work with and very versatile, lending themselves to both sweet and savoury dishes.

FISH
Blue-eye also known as deep sea trevalla or trevally and blue eye cod; thick, moist, white-fleshed fish.

Ling also known as pink ling, rock ling and kingclip; this large member of the cod family is usually sold in thick, firm, skinless fillets.
Snapper small, firm-fleshed, distinct-tasting fish sold whole, good for any kind of cooking method; a number of varieties include red, pink and yellowtail snapper.

FISH SAUCE also called nam pla or nuoc nam; made from pulverised salted fermented fish, most often anchovies. Has a pungent smell and strong taste; use sparingly. There are many kinds, of varying intensity.

GARAM MASALA a blend of spices, originating in North India; based on varying proportions of cardamom, cinnamon, cloves, coriander, fennel and cumin, roasted and ground together. Black pepper and chilli can be added.

damper

pide

pitta

flour tortilla

bruschetta

GREEN PEPPERCORNS soft, unripe berry of the pepper plant usually sold packed in brine (occasionally found dried, packed in salt). Distinctive fresh taste that goes well with mustard or cream sauces.

GRIDDLE-FRY term that describes cooking in or on a non-oiled, flat, cast-iron pan over high heat. Some griddle pans have non-stick coatings, some have ridges in the base that suggest barbecue or grill patterns on the cooked food.

KUMARA Polynesian name of an orange-fleshed sweet potato often incorrectly called a yam.

LAMB
Fillet tenderloin; the smaller piece of meat from a row of loin chops or cutlets.
French-trimmed lamb shanks also known as drumsticks or Frenched shanks; all the gristle and narrow end of the shank (forequarter leg) bone is discarded and the remaining meat trimmed.

LEMON PEPPER SEASONING a blend of crushed black peppercorns, lemon, herbs and spices.

MARINARA SEAFOOD MIX a mixture of uncooked, chopped seafood.

MUSTARD
Black, seeds also known as brown mustard seeds; more pungent than the white (or yellow) seeds used in most prepared mustards.
Dijon a pale brown, distinctively flavoured fairly mild French mustard.
Mild English less pungent version of traditional hot English mustard.
Powder finely ground white (yellow) mustard seeds.
Seeded also known as wholegrain. A flavourful coarse-grain mustard made from crushed mustard seeds and Dijon-style mustard.

NOODLES
Hokkien also known as stir-fry noodles; fresh wheat flour noodles resembling thick, yellow-brown spaghetti that

do not require pre-cooking before being used.
Rice vermicelli also known as rice-flour or rice-stick noodles; made from ground rice. Sold dried, are best either deep-fried or soaked then stir-fried or used in soups.

NUTS
Pine also known as pignoli; small, cream-coloured kernels obtained from the cones of certain pine trees.
Pistachio pale green, delicately flavoured nut inside hard off-white shells. To peel, soak shelled nuts in boiling water for about 5 minutes; drain, then pat dry with absorbent paper. Rub skins with cloth to peel.

OIL
Olive mono-unsaturated; pressed from tree-ripened olives. Good for everyday cooking and as an ingredient.
Peanut pressed from ground peanuts; most commonly used oil in Asian cooking because of its high smoke point.

OYSTER SAUCE Asian in origin, this rich, brown sauce is made from oysters and brine, cooked with salt and soy sauce, and thickened with starches.

PANZANELLA Traditional Italian salad based around bread soaked in water, anchovies and assorted fresh vegetables and olives.

PAPRIKA ground dried red capsicum (bell pepper), available sweet or hot.

PASTA
Fettuccine ribbon pasta averaging 5mm in width, made from durum wheat semolina and egg, available fresh or dried, plain or flavoured with various herbs, pepper or vegetable essences.
Fusilli little corkscrew shaped, or twisted, pasta.
Gnocchi Italian "dumplings" made of potatoes, semolina or flour; can be boiled in water or baked with cheese or sauce.
Penne translates literally as "quills"; ridged macaroni cut diagonally into short lengths.

PASTA SAUCE, BOTTLED a prepared tomato-based sauce (sometimes called sugo or ragu on the label).

PIDE (Turkish bread) comes in long (about 45cm) flat loaves as well as individual rounds; made from wheat flour and sprinkled with sesame or black onion seeds.

PITTA (Lebanese bread) also spelled pita, this wheat-flour pocket bread is sold in large, flat pieces that separate easily into 2 paper-thin rounds. Also available in small thick pieces called **Pocket Pitta**.

POACH a cooking method where food is simmered in liquid (water, stock, etc).

PLUM SAUCE a thick, sweet and sour dipping sauce made from plums, vinegar, sugar, chillies and spices.

POLENTA a flour-like cereal made of ground corn (maize); similar to cornmeal but coarser and darker in colour; also the name of the dish made from it.

PORK NECK sometimes called pork scotch; boneless cut from the foreloin.

PRAWNS also called shrimp.

PROSCIUTTO salted-cured, air-dried (unsmoked) pressed ham; usually sold in paper-thin slices, ready to eat.

QUAIL small, delicate flavoured, domestically grown game birds ranging in weight from 250g to 300g; also known as partridge.

READY-ROLLED PUFF PASTRY sheets of frozen puff pastry.

REDCURRANT JELLY a preserve made from redcurrants used as a glaze for desserts and meats.

REFRIED BEANS pinto beans (similar to borlotti), cooked twice: soaked and boiled then mashed and fried, traditionally in lard. A Mexican staple, "frijoles refritos" or refried beans are available canned in supermarkets. **Mexe-Beans** is a trade name for canned pinto beans in chilli sauce.

RICE
Arborio small, round-grain rice well-suited to absorb a large amount of liquid; especially suitable for risottos.
Calrose a medium-grain variety that is extremely versatile; can substitute for short- or long-grain rice when necessary.

RICE FLOUR a very fine flour made from ground white rice.

SATAY SAUCE traditional Indonesian/Malaysian spicy peanut sauce served with grilled meat skewers.

SAUSAGES
Chorizo Spanish in origin, a highly seasoned spicy salami made from ground pork, garlic and red peppers.
Csabai Hungarian in origin, a dried pork or beef sausage flavoured with pimiento, paprika and peppercorns.
Pepperoni thin, long air-dried Italian sausage made of minced pork, beef, additional fat and black and red pepper.

SCALLOPS bivalve molluscs with fluted shell; we used them with coral (roes) attached.

SEMOLINA Made from durum wheat milled into various textured granules, from fine to coarse. The main ingredient in good pastas, in some kinds of gnocchi and in Middle-Eastern and Indian sweets.

SESAME SEEDS Black and white are the most common of the oval seeds harvested from the tropical plant *Sesamum indicum*; however there are red and brown varieties also. Used in za'atar, halva and tahini. To toast: spread seeds evenly on oven tray, toast in moderate oven briefly.

SOY SAUCE made from fermented soy beans. Several variations are available, among them are salt-reduced, light, sweet and salty.

SPATCHCOCK a small chicken (poussin), no more than 6 weeks old, weighing a maximum 500g.

SUGAR we use coarse granulated table sugar, also known as crystal sugar.
Brown an extremely soft, fine granulated sugar retaining its molasses flavour.

SUMAC a purple-red, astringent spice ground from berries growing on shrubs native to the Mediterranean; adds a tart, lemony flavour to barbecued meats.

TABASCO SAUCE brand name of an extremely fiery sauce made from vinegar, hot red peppers and salt.

TABOULLEH Traditional Lebanese salad consisting mainly of large amounts of chopped fresh parsley with fresh mint and burghul.

TACO SEASONING MIX a packaged seasoning meant to duplicate the Mexican sauce made from oregano, cumin, chillies and other spices.

TAHINI a rich, buttery paste made from sesame seeds.

TOMATO
Paste triple-concentrated tomato puree used to flavour soups, stews, sauces, etc.
Puree canned pureed tomatoes (not tomato paste). Substitute with fresh peeled and pureed tomatoes.
Sauce also known as ketchup or catsup; a flavoured condiment made from tomatoes, vinegar and spices.

TORTILLA thin, round unleavened bread originating in Mexico; can be made at home or purchased frozen, fresh or vacuum-packed. Two kinds are available, one made from wheat flour and the other from corn (maizemeal). This word, when used in Spanish as opposed to Mexican kitchens, is the name for omelette, usually filled with potatoes.

TZATZIKI Greek yogurt and cucumber dish sometimes containing mint and/or garlic.

VINEGAR
Balsamic authentic only from the province of Modena, Italy; made from a regional wine of white Trebbiano grapes specially processed then aged in antique wooden casks to give its exquisite pungent flavour.

WORCESTERSHIRE SAUCE thin, dark-brown spicy sauce used as a condiment and seasoning for meat, gravies, etc.

YELLOW BABY SQUASH also known as pattipan, scallopine or summer squash; small, flattish yellow or green thin-skinned squash.

YELLOW SPLIT PEAS a legume; also known as field peas.

YOGURT a plain, unflavoured full-fat yogurt.

ZUCCHINI also known as courgette.

couscous

semolina

burghul

barley

polenta

felafel mix

INDEX

MAKE YOUR OWN STOCK

Recipes can be made 4 days ahead: store, covered, in refrigerator; or freeze in smaller quantities. Remove any fat from the surface after stock has been refrigerated overnight.

Stock is available in cans or tetra packs. If using stock cubes or powder, use 1 teaspoon of stock powder or 1 small cube with 1 cup (250ml) water to give a strong stock. Check salt and fat content of packaged stocks.
Recipes make 2.5 litres (10 cups).

BEEF STOCK

2kg meaty beef bones
2 medium (300g) onions
2 celery sticks, chopped
2 medium (250g) carrots, chopped
3 bay leaves
2 teaspoons black peppercorns
5 litres (20 cups) water
3 litres (12 cups) water, extra

Place bones and unpeeled chopped onions in baking dish. Bake in hot oven about 1 hour or until bones and onions are well browned. Transfer bones and onions to large pan, add celery, carrots, bay leaves, peppercorns and water; simmer, uncovered, 3 hours. Add extra water, simmer, uncovered, further 1 hour; strain.

FISH STOCK

1.5kg fish bones
3 litres (12 cups) water
1 medium (150g) onion, chopped
2 sticks celery, chopped
2 bay leaves
1 teaspoon black peppercorns

Combine all ingredients in large pan, simmer, uncovered, 20 minutes; strain.

CHICKEN STOCK

2kg chicken bones
2 medium (300g) onions, chopped
2 celery sticks, chopped
2 medium (250g) carrots, chopped
3 bay leaves
2 teaspoons black peppercorns
5 litres (20 cups) water

Combine all ingredients in large pan, simmer, uncovered, 2 hours; strain.

VEGETABLE STOCK

2 large (360g) carrots, chopped
2 large (360g) parsnips, chopped
4 medium (600g) onions, chopped
12 celery sticks, chopped
4 bay leaves
2 teaspoons black peppercorns
6 litres (24 cups) water

Combine all ingredients in large pan, simmer, uncovered, 1½ hours; strain.

FACTS AND FIGURES

Wherever you live, you'll be able to use our recipes with the help of these easy-to-follow conversions. While these conversions are approximate only, the difference between an exact and the approximate conversion of various liquid and dry measures is but minimal and will not affect your cooking results.

DRY MEASURES

Metric	Imperial
15g	1/2oz
30g	1oz
60g	2oz
90g	3oz
125g	4oz (1/4lb)
155g	5oz
185g	6oz
220g	7oz
250g	8oz (1/2lb)
280g	9oz
315g	10oz
345g	11oz
375g	12oz (3/4lb)
410g	13oz
440g	14oz
470g	15oz
500g	16oz (1lb)
750g	24oz (1 1/2lb)
1kg	32oz (2lb)

LIQUID MEASURES

Metric	Imperial
30ml	1 fluid oz
60ml	2 fluid oz
100ml	3 fluid oz
125ml	4 fluid oz
150ml	5 fluid oz (1/4 pint/1 gill)
190ml	6 fluid oz
250ml	8 fluid oz
300ml	10 fluid oz (1/2 pint)
500ml	16 fluid oz
600ml	20 fluid oz (1 pint)
1000ml (1 litre)	1 3/4 pints

HELPFUL MEASURES

Metric	Imperial
3mm	1/8in
6mm	1/4in
1cm	1/2in
2cm	3/4in
2.5cm	1in
5cm	2in
6cm	2 1/2in
8cm	3in
10cm	4in
13cm	5in
15cm	6in
18cm	7in
20cm	8in
23cm	9in
25cm	10in
28cm	11in
30cm	12in (1ft)

MEASURING EQUIPMENT

The difference between one country's measuring cups and another's is, at most, within a 2 or 3 teaspoon variance. (For the record, 1 Australian metric measuring cup holds approximately 250ml.) The most accurate way of measuring dry ingredients is to weigh them. When measuring liquids, use a clear glass or plastic jug with the metric markings.

If you would like to purchase The Australian Women's Weekly Test Kitchen's metric measuring cups and spoons (as approved by Standards Australia), turn to page 120 for details and order coupon. You will receive:

- a graduated set of 4 cups for measuring dry ingredients, with sizes marked on the cups.
- a graduated set of 4 spoons for measuring dry and liquid ingredients, with amounts marked on the spoons.
- 1 teaspoon: 5ml
- 1 tablespoon: 20ml.

Note: North America and UK use 15ml tablespoons. All cup and spoon measurements are level.

How To Measure

When using graduated metric measuring cups, shake dry ingredients loosely into the appropriate cup. Do not tap the cup on a bench or tightly pack the ingredients unless directed to do so. Level top of measuring cups and measuring spoons with a knife. When measuring liquids, place a clear glass or plastic jug with metric markings on a flat surface to check accuracy at eye level.

We use large eggs having an average weight of 60g.

OVEN TEMPERATURES

These oven temperatures are only a guide. Always check the manufacturer's manual.

	C° (Celsius)	F° (Fahrenheit)	Gas Mark
Very slow	120	250	1
Slow	150	300	2
Moderately slow	160	325	3
Moderate	180 - 190	350 - 375	4
Moderately hot	200 - 210	400 - 425	5
Hot	220 - 230	450 - 475	6
Very hot	240 - 250	500 - 525	7

Life's easier with these great Home Library gifts

Protect your favourite cookbooks and keep them clean, tidy and within easy reach with this smart vinyl folder*. PLUS you can follow our recipes perfectly with a set of measuring cups and spoons, as used in the Women's Weekly Test Kitchen.

TO ORDER YOUR BOOK HOLDER OR MEASURING SET:

Price: Book Holder $11.95 (Australia); elsewhere $A21.95.
Metric Measuring Set $5.95 (Australia); $A8.00 (New Zealand); $A9.95 elsewhere
*prices include postage and handling. This offer is available in all countries.

Phone: Have your credit card details ready. Sydney: (02) 9260 0035; **elsewhere in Australia:** 1800 252 515 (free call, Mon-Fri, 8.30am-5.30pm) or FAX your order to (02) 9267 4363 or MAIL your order by photocopying or completing the coupon below.

Payment: **Australian residents:** we accept the credit cards listed, money orders and cheques. **Overseas residents:** we accept the credit cards listed, drafts in $A drawn on an Australian bank, and also British, New Zealand and U.S. cheques in the currency of the country of issue. Credit card charges are at the exchange rate current at the time of payment.

Complete coupon and fax or post to:
AWW Home Library Reader Offer, ACP Direct, PO Box 7036, Sydney NSW 1028.